Books by Sigurd F. Olson

SIGURD F. OLSON'S WILDERNESS DAYS (1972)

OPEN HORIZONS (1969)

RUNES OF THE NORTH (1963)

THE LONELY LAND (1961)

LISTENING POINT (1958)

THE SINGING WILDERNESS (1956)

These are BORZOI BOOKS
published by ALFRED A. KNOPF *in New York*

LISTENING POINT

Sigurd F. Olson

LISTENING

New York

Illustrations by Francis Lee Jaques

POINT

Alfred A. Knopf *1974*

L. C. Catalog card number: 58-10971
© Sigurd F. Olson, 1958

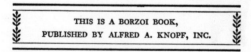

THIS IS A BORZOI BOOK,
PUBLISHED BY ALFRED A. KNOPF, INC.

Published September 22, 1958
Reprinted Seven Times
Ninth Printing, July 1974

To

all who have found Listening Points of their own

and to those who are still searching

ACKNOWLEDGMENTS

I AM DEEPLY GRATEFUL FOR criticism, editing, and encouragement to Ann Langen and Florence Peterson of Ely, to Jean and Fred Packard of Washington, D.C., and to my family, especially my wife, Elizabeth.

My deep appreciation goes to Francis Lee Jaques for his superb sketches for *Listening Point.*

For professional advice and counsel on chapters of scientific and historical interest, I am indebted to Mr. John Dobie of the Minnesota Conservation Department, St. Paul; Dr. Olga

ACKNOWLEDGMENTS

Lakela, Botany Department, University of Minnesota at Duluth; Sigurd T. Olson, Fish and Wildlife Service, Fairbanks, Alaska; Clair F. Rollings, Fish and Wildlife Service, St. Paul; Milton Stenlund, Minnesota Conservation Department, Grand Rapids; Dr. Grace Lee Nute, History Departments, Hamline and Macalester Colleges, Minneapolis; Dr. G. M. Schwartz and Dr. George Thiel, Geology Department, University of Minnesota; Dr. William Marshall, Department of Economic Zoology, University of Minnesota.

The quotation used in "Young Ottertail" came from W. H. Hudson's *Days of My Boyhood*.

Lewis O. Shelley's vivid description of the soaring of the broad-wings was taken from *Life Histories of North American Birds of Prey*, by Arthur Cleveland Bent.

CONTENTS

ix

CONTENTS

LISTENING POINT

CHAPTER I

LISTENING POINT

LISTENING POINT is a bare glaciated spit of rock in the Quetico-Superior country. Each time I have gone there I have found something new which has opened up great realms of thought and interest. For me it has been a point of discovery and, like all such places of departure, has assumed meaning far beyond the ordinary.

From it I have seen the immensity of space and glimpsed

at times the grandeur of creation. There I have sensed the span of uncounted centuries and looked down the path all life has come. I have explored on this rocky bit of shore the great concept that nothing stands alone and everything, no matter how small, is part of a greater whole. The point has shown me time and again that William Blake was right when he wrote:

> *To see the world in a grain of sand,*
> *And a heaven in a wild flower;*
> *Hold infinity in the palm of your hand,*
> *And eternity in an hour.*

I believe that what I have known there is one of the oldest satisfactions of man, that when he gazed upon the earth and sky with wonder, when he sensed the first vague glimmerings of meaning in the universe, the world of knowledge and spirit was opened to him. While we are born with curiosity and wonder and our early years full of the adventure they bring, I know such inherent joys are often lost. I also know that, being deep within us, their latent glow can be fanned to flame again by awareness and an open mind.

Listening Point is dedicated to recapturing this almost forgotten sense of wonder and learning from rocks and trees and all the life that is found there, truths that can encompass all. Through a vein of rose quartz at its tip can be read the geological history of the planet, from an old pine stump the ecological succession of the plant kingdom, from an Indian legend the story of the dreams of all mankind.

4

For a long time I had looked for such a place, explored the country within reach of home for some spot that held what I wanted, and I wanted many things. There should be sunsets and moonrises and northern lights, a little beach and water that was crystal clear, glaciated rocks, a level spot for a tent, and a place for a cabin too. Above all, there should be vistas into wide open space, loons with the dusk full of their calling, seagulls screaming in the mornings and the long lazy sweep of them as they come in to feed. Such things were important to the purpose I had in mind, for through their magic I would be more aware and alive and sense what I had known on many exploring expeditions of the past.

One day after a long search I found my point. I had come through woods and swamps off the end of a road and was suddenly out of the brush and trees on an open shelf of rock. There it was as I had dreamed, a composite picture of all the places in the north that I had known and loved. I stood there for a long time, then walked over the gray ledges to the end of the point. Its tip faced the west, and across a mile of open water were clusters of rocky pine-clad islands with narrow channels between them.

Then I saw the campsite, a flat patch of bearberry on a shelf above the water's edge, high enough to be safe from the waves, a place I would have chosen with joy on any canoe trip I had ever been on. Here I could roll up in my sleeping-bag and feel I was still far in the bush.

The crest of the point was smooth, but fringing it all around were the pines, the gnarled wind-swept ones, the twisted weather-beaten specimens for whom life had been hard, some of them a century of age and still no bigger than a post. Back of the crest was a game trail leading through a colonnade of tall trees toward the ridges in the east.

I discovered there was not only one glaciated spit of rock but several. They lay like an open hand, with the widespread thumb holding a crescent bay between it and the palm. The fingers were half closed, the middle one facing the sunsets, the index the moonrises, the little finger the wild free expanses of the north channel.

I followed the deer trail through the pines and down to the bay. There was just a chance that the southwest winds of thousands of years might have had their effect on the rocks of that little cove. It was screened by a fringe of alder and willow, but when I stepped onto a flat rock beyond them, there was a tiny strip of white sand sloping gradually into the deep and the water so clear I could see the ripple marks far out from shore. Sheltered from the cold northwest gales, the little bay would always be warm and swimming a joy.

The end of the thumb was a bold rocky ledge with a pine tree standing there alone. I started over there and halfway found a stand of Norway pines and clusters of white birch scattered among huge craggy rocks. From the top of one of them I could see the beach and the point itself and the vistas across to the islands and knew the search was over. Here was everything I had ever hoped to find. I would never own the water or the horizons, but the sunsets, the moonrises and the vistas would belong as much to me as though written into the deed itself.

I felt rich that day with my good fortune. Though it might soon be mine, I realized that even so I would be a tenant leasing the enjoyment of this bit of the earth's crust for a few short years. The point had seen the Indians and voyageurs, the prospectors and loggers, had been a stopping-place for countless travelers long before I found it. They had seen its storms and northern lights and had watched its vistas before I came.

From this one place I would explore the entire north and all life, including my own. I could look to the stars and feel that here was a focal point of great celestial triangles, a point as important as any one on the planet. For me it would be a listening-post from which I might even hear the music of the spheres.

Wilderness sounds would be here, bird songs in the mornings and at dusk. The aspen leaves would whisper and the pines as well, and in the sound of water and wind I would hear all that is worth listening for. I would come in all seasons, when the first buds of spring were painting the hillsides, when the sounds of summer made it seem as though the woods were pulsating with life. I would be here in the autumns watching the pageantry of color, in the winter when the lake was frozen and still and the point deep with snow. I would come to listen and feel and to recapture for a little while the old joys I had known.

I must leave it as beautiful as I found it. Nothing must ever happen there that might detract in the slightest from what it now had. I would enjoy it and discover all that was to be found there and learn as time went on that here perhaps was all I might ever hope to know.

As I sat there on the rock I realized that, in spite of the closeness of civilization and the changes that hemmed it in, this remnant of the old wilderness would speak to me of silence and solitude, of belonging and wonder and beauty. Though the point was only a small part of the vastness reaching far to the arctic, from it I could survey the whole. While it would be mine for only a short time, this glaciated shore with its twisted trees and caribou moss would grow into my life and into the lives of all who shared it with me.

I named this place Listening Point because only when one comes to listen, only when one is aware and still, can things be seen and heard. Everyone has a listening-point somewhere. It does not have to be in the north or close to the wilderness, but some place of quiet where the universe can be contemplated with awe. The chapters that follow are simply the stories of what I have found on my particular point of departure. The adventures that have been mine can be known by anyone.

CHAPTER 2

BEARBERRY LEDGE

C AMPSITES in the north are chosen for the things you can see at a distance, a landing for the canoe and outfit and a place for the tent. But they are loved and remembered for the things you cannot see. Not until you have gone ashore and been there awhile do these

9

other values make themselves known; not until the furor of pitching camp is through and supper well under way is there any awareness of the subtle undertones of any place. Only then, when there is nothing more to do than tend the fire or look to the horizons, do the permanent values grow into one's consciousness.

At the end of any trip, when the country as a whole is a grand panorama of lakes and portages, of rapids and falls, of storms and quiet, and constantly shifting vistas that all seem to merge into one, it is certain campsites, what happened there and how they made you feel, that stand out more clearly than the rest. Most vivid of all are the new ones, those you carved out of the bush and where no one had ever camped before. All discoveries there seem important—the actual location of the fireplace and the tent, silhouettes of certain rocks and trees, the way the water swirled in an eddy, how a moose sloshed into a bay and stood there undisturbed.

And so when the time came to spend our first night on the point, to dedicate the bearberry ledge, the composite of all the campsites we had known, knowing these things, we were expectant and aware. Conditions must be ideal for our first night out, for we would return again and again and build upon what we had found there. While as old voyageurs we could enjoy it in the rain or in the teeth of a gale, this time we wanted a combination of all the best that could happen. We had a choice, could pick the perfect night, wait if necessary and plan our expedition so that everything we dreamed of might be there.

So we chose a time of the full moon, a soft evening when it would come up orange and mellow over the little bay and the black ridges behind the beach. We wanted a sunset too, and that meant wisps of clouds and possibly a thunderhead for grandeur. It should be a night when we were alone, so we could go without a word to absorb the feelings that were there.

The first night of the full moon was against us, for in the afternoon a strong wind whipped out of the north and the sky was suddenly full of angry scudding clouds. The second was ideal, and we made swift preparations to go, packed the sleeping-bags, the tent, some coffee and tea, and something for supper and breakfast. But just as we were ready to take off, the house filled with guests and the bearberry patch was forgotten.

The third night and the last when the moon was really full, we were alone. There were wisps of clouds in the west, a few high cumulus peaks above them, and a soft zephyr of a breeze out of the south. The paddle down was quiet as a prayer, reflections rode the shorelines, and rocky points lay like giant spears along the water. Where we passed the birches, they shimmered and shook as the ripples of the canoe went over them. A seagull sitting out in the open seemed twice as large as it should be; it floated on the surface like a patch of foam. We passed the narrows at Gregories, Dollar Island, and Kaleva Bay, and there just a mile away lay the point, its smooth gray finger of rock with its fringe of little pines waiting our invasion.

Even at a distance I would have picked such a spot and paddled far out of my way to reach it. But this time we knew what was there. All we didn't know were the things the night could give, sights and sounds and smells that are known only when one sleeps out of doors. The sun was already low, and in the open reaches the color was beginning to show.

We landed the canoe on the smooth flat rock and carried the packs to the place where the bearberry lay in a tightly packed mat over the ledge, the same resilient cover one finds clear to the Arctic Circle and beyond. The hard little stems with their tiny oval leaves were interlaced so tightly that the ground beneath could not be seen. No sticks, pine needles or dust lay upon it. It was fresh, wind-blown and clean, a proper place for a night as important as this. The point was as undisturbed as though we had paddled all day and were far to the north.

Because it was clear we did not pitch the tent, just laid it on the ground and placed our bags on top as we had done many times in the past. There might be dew, but this night we wanted the stars and the moonlight. We built a small fireplace at the very tip of the point, kindled a blaze with a handful of needles, and put the kettle on to boil. It was very quiet there, and suddenly we realized not a word had been spoken since we landed.

After supper we paddled off into the darkening cluster of islands, slipped into rocky channels colored with the sunset glow, drifted between them as lost to the sounds of the world as we had ever been. We caught a couple of small bass as we paddled along and a great northern too, which we released. The bass were enough for breakfast.

We passed several round glaciated knobs covered with caribou moss and stopped before a slender ridge of an island with a boulder big as a house tucked into a stand of Norway pine. The last rays of the sunset tinted the great boles of the trees and made them glow with fire. To that boulder the trees were as grass. It lay among them huge and gray and permanent, had been there thousands of years before they came, would be there long after they were gone.

We turned then and paddled back, drifted along listening to the loons and watched the sunset melt into the darkness of the ridges. The thunderhead had climbed high and was pink and white and silvered along its edges. As it moved toward the east, it changed to rose and mauve and then to blood red and purple. The west was now in full color and the water as well, and the spruces etched themselves against the horizon. In the east a low bank of cloud was brightening along its upper edge. We would have to hurry if we were to see the moon rise, so sped across the open water to the point, ran up the slope to the watching-place above the campsite. There on the rounded knob with its corydalis and caribou moss, we settled down to wait. The cloud began to glow, and then the first shining rim of the moon sliced through it. Swiftly it was out and full, great and golden and pulsating. The beach was silver now with a path of light that reached out tremulously toward the point. Behind us the west was still alive and the water opalescent, but soon the path of the moon would cut across it and its purple turn to silver and then to black. The point, which curved slightly toward the south, now held the glistening bay in the crook of its arm.

We watched for an hour until the moon was bright enough to guide us down the trail to the beach. Its light filtered through the pines, and the aspen were traceries of black on silver. In the bay itself, it was dark and no moon showed above the cedars that crowded close. I touched a match to a shred of birchbark, and the little fire that was laid there waiting for this night leaped into the dark. I fed the flames, and they burned as only cedar can, bright and yellow, spitting sparks high above them.

An hour later we were in our bags watching the moon come through the tops of the pines and listening to the lapping of waves against the rocks. The last I remembered was the silhouette of a gnarled little pine against the moon. No one, I thought, must ever touch that tree, no one ever change its twisted black against the sky. What storms it had withstood, how bravely it flaunted its few clumps of needles, how it had fought over the years for the right to live, thrusting its roots deep into the cracks of granite and greenstone beneath it, holding fast and desperately there as the storms from the northwest tried to tear it from its mooring.

Several tall and beautiful pines stood in the little valley at the base of the point. While stately and magnificent themselves, they had not the character of the small one just above, none of the hardness that typified the whole Canadian Shield. The Shield that covers most of the north with volcanic rock is unyielding and ancient, means muskeg and forest, and cold and storm, and violent roaring rivers. It has spirit and challenge, and the little pine was the embodiment of it all.

I awoke during the middle of the night and lay there watching the stars. They were bright and close, and Mars hung like a lantern in the east, and I could see the Pleiades and Cassiopeia, the Big Dipper and a million more, and the Milky Way lying across the sky like a great stippled roadway paved with countless pinpoints of light.

A loon called, one long mournful note, and a bird cheeped plaintively from the Indian plum back of the campsite. The whitethroat started its long thin note bravely, then stopped in the middle as though suddenly realizing it wasn't daylight after all, but only the light of the moon.

Then I was conscious of a sound I had forgotten, the soft rushing of the rapids in the Burntside River a mile to the south. Years before in the dead of winter I had come up the river and skirted the open water, but had forgotten it was close enough to the point so it could be heard on a quiet night. At times the sound seemed to ebb and flow, then disappeared entirely. But there was no mistake, a rapids had come with the point, music in the quiet of the night when a soft south wind was there to carry it. Someday we would take the canoe and paddle down there, explore the rapids again and push through the rice beds just below.

We were up just as the sun was peeking over the hill in back of the beach. The moon was far in the west, had lost its whiteness and turned again to orange. The birds were in full song, and a flock of loons chased each other madly across the water. Instinctively I looked toward the river mouth, and there they were, the mists, the galloping white horses of all river mouths in the north beginning their run toward the open range of the lake.

We watched them with joy, for this we had not counted on, something extra that not all campsites have, only those near the mouths of rivers or deep marshy bays. We walked to the top of the point, and there in the bay were the horses too, pink and white in the light of the rising sun. It was warm, so we plunged in and swam through the mists to the beach and back again and had our breakfast watching them disappear as the sun climbed high. A voyageur's breakfast was ours, bread and fried bass, coffee and a handful of blueberries picked off the rocks behind us. How good to sit there in the sun and bask after our swim, how rich the smell of coffee in the morning, how sweet the fish we had caught among the islands.

We had spent our first night on the point, dedicated it to all the campsites we had known, to all the memories of wilderness expeditions of the past. We had watched a sunset and a moonrise too, had seen the stars and the silhouette of the little pine against the moon. We had heard a rapids far off and the lap of waves again and the midnight call of a startled whitethroat. We had watched the horses of the mists and enjoyed a breakfast that would have gladdened the heart of any traveler in the bush. The bearberry ledge of Listening Point was a campsite we would love and remember always.

CHAPTER 3

THE CABIN

ROM the very beginning of
our adventure with the point, we had dreamed of someday
having a little cabin tucked back in the pines, a place we
could come to on a moment's notice without having to
bother with food and equipment; a simple shelter where we
could just move in, spend a few hours, a night or two, or if

in the mood even a week, an outpost away from the phone and interruptions.

It must be as natural as a shelter back in the bush, like an overhanging ledge or a lean-to, or a cabin on some trapper's route. We would carry water from the lake, cut our firewood, do all the things we would have done in the wilds, and when we went to sleep at night we wanted the feeling we were still close to the out-of-doors and that the cabin was not merely an extension of our house in town.

We wanted the partridge to walk around it, to come out in the dusk and sit there in the twilight unafraid. We wanted red squirrels spiraling down the trunks of the pines and vaulting onto the roof as though it were part of the trees themselves. Even the deer mice would be welcome to build their nests in some dark corner under the rafters. The chickadees would be part of it, and the soft warbling notes of the whiskey-jacks, and the calling of the loons on the open lake. The wind and the waves and all the sounds of the night would be there. It must be only one room, just large enough for a couple of bunks, a fireplace and a table, as close to the primitive as we could keep it and in harmony with Listening Point.

At first we thought of placing it out on the point itself, on the flat spot that lies like the hollow of a cupped hand back of the fringe of dwarf pines that border the sides. There it would be high enough to catch the vistas and have the feeling of space all around. But the more we thought about it, the more we were convinced it would be wrong, for nothing must ever change the point itself; it must remain a sanctuary forever, a place reserved for vistas and dreams and long thoughts. Even a gray weathered cabin that blended so closely with the rocks and caribou moss that it seemed a part of them would inevitably result in changes there.

So we began to look around, to explore the shoreline for other possibilities. Just to the north and back of one of the minor points was a stand of pines with a smooth rocky shelf from which we could catch the sweep of the lake to the islands and also the north channel. That place would be cool all summer long and there would be shade, but it faced the gales of autumn and spring, and in the winter there would be no protection either for us or for the birds.

In the north the summer months are short, and we would be there in all seasons. When the warm weather is gone, what really counts is the sun. So we looked to the south below the pines and the shelf of rock where a huge glacial boulder had been dropped by the ice. I had always liked that boulder and the way it sat so solidly at the base of the point as though it were a commanding monument marking a frontier, a line beyond which one must never go. The boulder guarded the point. Until that moment we had never thought of building there, for it was too sheltered to get the full sweep of the horizons other locations offered, but with the boulder marking the place, the choice was made for us. The ground was level; the cabin door would face the bay and the trail leading up to the main point. While there would be no unbroken views from the windows, they would give us a hint of what could be seen by merely stepping out of doors.

I have always felt that views through windows leave much to be desired, that to really enjoy a view it should be undimmed by glass or frame. While a scene might be beautiful from the inside, something important is always lost there, for a vista divorced from the open air and the smells and sounds and feelings around you is only partially enjoyed. If we could see all there was to see from indoors, if we became content to have the beauty around us encompassed by the four walls of the cabin, we would lose what we came to find, and that we must never do.

Above the boulder was a low ridge that gave protection from the storms and from foreign sounds that during the summer might come from the lake. Just to the south was a bare slope with bracken fern growing upon it, a slope that gradually led to the shore not fifty feet away. I could picture that slope in the spring when the snows began to melt, how it would turn brown much more swiftly than any other place, be warm and dry long before the solid drifts under the pines had begun to settle, and how the chickadees and nuthatches would enjoy it all winter long. On the open point of the ledge above, there was little shelter and far more shade than they would like. Here was the south slope of a protected ridge, and even in the depths of winter, while the mercury was far below zero, it would get warm enough at high noon for some to try their mating-calls months ahead of time. It would be good to sit there during the first warm days of spring and watch the ice in the bay turn black and open spots of blue begin to appear.

It was the sun as much as the boulder that sold us on the site, and we were happy with our choice. Back of it were windfalls and wood for the future; we could chop there to make a woodpile and not be concerned with what we were doing to the point. Furthermore, did not the big boulder mark the place beyond which we could not go? The cabin would nestle close to it and to the slope with its bank of pines, and in the fall a maple would flame against the logs. We could run to the water, plunge in, swim to the beach and back, and warm ourselves on the sunny side.

We wanted a cabin that blended into its surroundings, a cabin as gray as the rocks themselves. The north country is full of old cabins built by the original Finnish and Scandinavian settlers when they first moved in. Many are now falling apart and being replaced by modern homes, but all of them have weathered a silvery gray, for none have ever known paint or varnish.

If we could find one of these cabins back in the clearings below the canoe country, one that was still sound, we would buy it, take it down log by log, and bring it to the point. Built of tamarack, jackpine, or cedar, with dovetailed corners, these cabins are so expertly hewn and the logs fit so closely together that little chinking is ever required. The result of centuries of building in Europe's north, they were designed to keep out the bitter winds. The new settlers brought their broadaxes with them, and, more than that, skills perfected by necessity. Such a cabin, it seemed to us, would fit the point, for it would have tradition behind it, and in its soft grayness there would be no jarring note.

We began to explore the countryside, drove down old logging roads into abandoned clearings, always watching for the telltale gray of old cabins and barns. We looked at many around Ely and in the Little Fork country to the northwest, but invariably the roofs were fallen in and the corners soft with decay. One day we found one built of jack-pine and in excellent condition, but the owner refused to sell.

"That cabin has no price," he said. "I was born there; my father built it, and there it will stand until I die."

That we understood.

Then in the Bear Island River country to the south, seven miles from home, we found exactly what we wanted, a cabin that had not been used for many years, with the roof still sound and the logs silvery gray. It was large enough, and I pictured it sitting next to the pines with the warm slope just below it. I approached the owner with caution, but, to my joy, there was only one question: "Why should anyone want to bother with an old-fashioned building like that?" I tried to explain, and that day came into possession of a cabin that met all of our requirements.

It seemed particularly fitting that it should have come from a country which long before had been on the route of settlers and voyageurs. Up from Lake Superior along the St. Louis River into the chain of waterways called Embarrass by the

French because of its difficulties, then into the Pike and Lake Vermillion, down the Tamarack to Burntside, then to the Kawishiwi and the mouth of the Bear Island to the south. Now one of these old cabins would follow the voyageurs, the settlers, and the loggers, would find a resting-place at the end of their trail.

After that day we began to plan. It would be some time before the cabin could be moved, time enough so we would know exactly how it should be before the actual rebuilding. A door must open toward the point and perhaps another to the south. Two windows would face the beach and two more the north. There would be two bunks, and bookshelves above the windows all along the four walls. We would build a sturdy table from an old dead cedar near by, and benches from a pine. Birch pegs would do for hanging clothes and equipment. A washstand would be outside, with a bucket and a towel, so the room itself would not be cluttered.

The fireplace would be built of native stone gathered down at the shore. We would build it ourselves out of the same rock that made up the point so it would blend into its background of greenstones, granites, and schists that were all around. It would be no higher than just above the peak of the roof, be broad and low, but the draft would be good because the winds would sweep from one side of the point to the other. It must take good logs that would burn a long time, have a hearth big enough so the blackened pots we used on our canoe trips could stand there and simmer with the heat. We could bake bannock there, and the old cooking outfit

23

would feel right at home. The woods were full of firewood begging to be used, and what a joy it would be on a cold rainy night to roll in and watch the glow of the coals; how swiftly the cabin would warm up in the morning with the waiting kindling that had been toasting there all night long.

We talked about a porch, but abandoned the idea. With windows looking over the water on the south and giving glimpses to the north, we needed no porch, and if we stepped outside we would have the feeling of a porch that encompassed the whole horizon. A porch would extend the cabin and mean a different roof. It would cut light from the windows on the side where it was placed and change the simple lines of the structure we had found.

We would build no boathouse either, for all we would own would be a canoe. We wanted the silences and had no use for larger craft. We could reach the islands in a few minutes of paddling and slip along the shores with nothing to detract from the quiet that was always there. When time came to store the canoe, we could tuck it under the broad eaves of the cabin, and there it could rest all winter long.

That cabin would be a symbol of a way of life, an extension of an ideal that was all involved with Listening Point. To violate that ideal would mean a sacrifice of what we really wanted there. The point, like the old wilderness, is a fragile thing in spite of its granitic hardness, in spite of the fact it withstood the ice sheet and the weathering ever since. It would be a part of the north, part of the wilderness, and within it would be the simplicity, the stark beauty and reality

24

of the forests of northern Europe from which it came. In those hand-hewn logs with their tight-mortised corners that through the centuries have made existence possible there, was a sense of belonging to a harsh and forbidding land. This it would never lose, for the north is the same wherever it might be.

CHAPTER 4

THE BREAKING

THE bulldozer roared down the highway with a clatter and shrieking of metal, came to a stop at the end where a narrow woods trail continued toward the lake. I had cut part of that trail a year before to within a few hundred feet of the cabin, knew every tree and shrub and rock all the way in, had done some grading with a rake and grub hoe in preparation for the day when the dozer would come to finish what was begun. But somehow I was unprepared for this, the noise and violence, and I looked at the huge orange monster with apprehension and dismay.

What would it do to the trees we had saved so carefully, to the clumps of mountain maple, the little spruces and balsams, the flowers and ferns and the gray lichen-covered boulders in its path? What about the mosses on the rocks of the old river bed down in the gully? What about the sidehill below the ridge where the sumac and the bracken grow? What would it do to the soil itself? At that moment I was uncertain and afraid. Perhaps it was wrong to build the road. Perhaps after all I should have approached the point by water as though it were an island or walked in from the highway almost a mile away. But when I thought of those who owned the land beyond me who would have built the road in any case, I knew there was no choice.

The cat-driver got off, looked the situation over, climbed back nonchalantly into his seat, shifted gears, and pushed against a clump of shining white birch. The clump went down and the tractor rode over it as though it were a tuft of grass, grinding the silver bark off the trunks, mashing the branches into the duff. After it was over, there they lay, scarred brown and twisted and covered with dirt, part of the road itself. A huge boulder lay in the way, a rounded granite mass of many tons. Dropped by glacial ice, it had lain there for thousands of years. Its top was covered with gray and green lichens, and a squirrel had peeled a cone there. The cat moved its enormous bulk against it, and it rolled easily to one side and the white raw granite underneath lay exposed to the light for the first time since its deposition. If only it could be turned up again so the lichens would show, but the engine roared on and I followed helplessly behind.

The great blade was lowered now. I watched it move down almost magically from its pushing position a foot or more above the surface to the level of the ground. A rounded hummock in the way was shoved into a depression and the road became level there. More boulders were moved out of the trail, and the din of screeching steel, the crash of stone against stone deafened all sounds of the forest. More trees went down, and it ground them into the duff. This was my road too, and I was appalled at what I had done.

Long ago I had watched a settler with a team and plow break a little clearing not far from the point, but somehow that had seemed a natural thing to do, as natural as hunting or fishing, cutting firewood or picking berries. This modern breaking of the soil seemed brutal by contrast, a violation and rape of the earth itself, steel against living tissue, sheer weight of mechanized metal against nature itself, something utterly devoid of feeling or sensibility.

As I watched the tractor forge ahead, widening turns, cutting down hills, and filling valleys, doing in one day what would have taken a man and his team a month to do, I knew that essentially there was no difference, for the end of both was the same. I could not help but compare that pioneer breaking of years ago with this.

That spring morning, how vividly it all came back to me now—snow in the hollows and on the north sides of hills, ground warm and brown under the sun, air full of the smells of resin, mold, and wetness, and along the river redwings singing from every bit of sedge. The river was blue and full, and creeks and rivulets gurgled everywhere on their way to join the flood. It was a great day, for the settler had worked long on his new clearing, grubbing out stumps and roots, leveling cradle knolls, carrying rocks to its edge. This was the hour of fulfillment.

I watched him hitch his team of grays to the breaking plow. They sensed the battle before them, pranced and plunged against the traces. A fanfare should have sounded then, a challenge to the four winds, but all I heard was the scream of a hawk in the blue, the warble of redwings in the marsh. There was no violence in that little clearing, no rending of steel against stone, no crashing of trees or grinding them into the dirt, though the cat-driver and the settler were one and the same, part of the pioneer tradition of building a civilization out of the wilds.

Across the clearing came a call. The horses threw their weight forward, and the sharp and shining steel bit into virgin soil. At times man and plow sprang into the air and the team backed, blowing and trembling, into the furrow. Again they plunged ahead, and the blade knifed through the tangle of sod and duff. They made the turn at the far end, and I watched their battling progress down the field. When they came to where I stood, sweat streaked their silver flanks and sides heaved.

"They like this breaking," said the farmer, mopping his forehead. "Did you see," he said proudly, "the way those grays laid into it?"

He clucked to his resting team and again they sprang forward, and suddenly the air was sweet with the smell of newly turned earth, and blackbirds and robins and killdeer were in the furrows picking up grubs and worms. As they turned away from me I seemed to see the joy of all men in working with the land, their fierce pride at giving something of value to the race, soil that for untold centuries had accumulated richness toward the time when they might take it for their own.

Since man abandoned his nomadic wanderings to till the soil, this had been his most vital task. He could go to war, build cities, harness atomic power, erect a civilization beyond his wildest dreams, but here, in the last analysis, was the front line of battle, here the rim of fire where he would live or die. The joy and basic satisfaction of the settler breaking his clearing and the cat-driver building my road was the same. Behind them both was the experience of the race. Only their method seemed different to me.

The cat was down in the valley now, pushing soil from the hillside to fill and cover a nest of boulders that once had been the bed of a past glacial stream. I followed behind it down the brown scar that was now the roadbed, looked sadly at the trees and rocks pushed so ruthlessly to the sides. Time would heal those scars, I knew, and in a year or so ferns and shrubs would crowd in from the edges and it would not seem as wide as now.

I stopped where the tractor had backed up the hillside to get some fill for a hole ahead, picked up a handful of dark topsoil. It was rich, and interlaced through it were rootlets and bits of leaves and little sticks. Not until this day had it seen the light. It had been accumulating there at the rate of an inch each thousand years, the humus so precious to the north. Within this handful of soil was a microbiotic community in balance, unseen bacteria, fungi, and viruses, each one necessary to the others and to all the plants and animals which grew above them, the result of a hundred centuries of adjustment and adaptation.

The cat was returning now, its tracks covered with mud from the swamp and littered with broken branches and leaves. It ground to a stop beside me, the great motor idling quietly.

"How'd you like it?" said the driver. "Sure looks different than it did this morning," and he turned to look back over the road he had built.

"You've done a good job," I said, dropping the handful of humus ahead of the track, but all I could see were the pines and birches and aspen that had gone down before him.

"You cut that trail pretty narrow," he said. "Had to widen it quite a bit in spots, but I was careful like you said."

I thanked him and waved as he shifted into gear and clanked off toward the highway and the trailer he had left there.

To him the job of road-building was good, the smell of new soil, the sharp pungence of steel biting into rock, the sense of enormous power that was his. When night came he could see what he had done, something necessary and worth while. My settler at the end of his day had plowed a clearing, the cat-driver broken a new road. For four hundred years Americans had been doing exactly that, taming a primeval continent, carving a future civilization from the raw resources of a land that had never before been touched.

Not long ago while flying across the country from Washington, D.C., to San Francisco I could not help but think of the land as it was at the time of discovery, when timber stood tall and straight along the coastal flats of the Atlantic, when forests reached clear to the Mississippi, herds of buffalo grazed the plains, and wildfowl darkened the sky. The continent was tamed now, with highways, power and oil lines enmeshing tightly the last remaining areas of the wild. There were dust bowls where once the prairies had bloomed, even abandoned farms; rivers clean and full a scant century before now were polluted or lying dry in the sun. Urban and industrial developments were spreading out along the highways until it was hard at times to tell where one city ended and another began.

Countless settlers with their breaking plows had made this possible. With their oxen and horses they had battled their way across the land, chopping, burning, making clearings, building roads and towns, and spreading out toward the Pacific. Those were days of freedom, hardship, and violence when men lived and died with the light of far horizons in their eyes.

Now there were no new lands to beckon restless men, but fleets of gigantic behemoths and tractors were altering the courses of rivers, leveling hills and filling valleys, building super highways across terrain that until now had been impassable. The age of the old pioneers was over, the days of homesteads, covered wagons, and "Westward Ho," but the era of the earth-movers had arrived and men were continuing the old tradition by changing the earth itself to suit their needs. While there was no more wilderness to conquer, there was land to be moved and remodeled to fit the pattern of a civilization still building.

I could hear the cat climbing onto its trailer, heard the great crash as it dropped into its steel bed for the ride back, then the sound of the truck going down the highway.

I hurried toward the point and reached it just in time to catch the last of the sunset. A hermit thrush nesting near the new road called as it had the evening before; incongruous that it could still be there after this day of violent sound and destruction, but there it was, and its clear violin notes sounded as sweetly ethereal as before.

The water was dark now, and a soft breeze moaned through the pines. A few miles to the south the settler was doing his chores, and the clearing he had made some years before was now a well-established field. In a little town not far away the cat-driver was having supper with his family, poring over a new map and pondering the adventure of another day.

I wondered, as I stood there watching black trunks against a flaming west, how long the old pioneer tradition would continue, if in the end all the Listening Points, all places of quiet and beauty would be altered by our unlimited ingenuity and enthusiasm for changing the face of the land.

CHAPTER 5

THE WITCHING HOUR

We were bass fishing, my
friend and I, and the canoe moved with scarcely a ripple
just outside the reeds. It was dusk, and the loons, hermit
thrushes, and whitethroats were almost through with their
calling. The tapered line unfurled and a fly soared over the
rushes, landing like a puff of down upon the water. It sat

there a moment, then seemed to struggle to free its wings before taking to the air. A swirl, and the fly rod bent, and soon the bass swam in slow wide circles beside me.

A swish of the net and it was inside, its red gills opening and closing, its tail beating a soft tattoo against the bottom of the canoe. Then again the rhythmic moving of the rod, the quiet drifting along the shore. My friend turned to me then from the bow and in his eyes was the light of magic. "The witching hour," he said.

I knew what he meant, for this was one of the times when the lake evoked a spell, when it mirrored not only the shores but the spirit as well. Through some strange alchemy that water possesses during such witching hours, we absorb its calm, its mystery or violence as though we were a part of it.

Millennia of living along seacoasts, lakes, and rivers, beside ponds and springs and waterholes have had their influence. Man's history is woven into waterways, for not only did he live beside them, but he used them as highways for hunting, exploration, and trade. Water assured his welfare, its absence meant migration or death, its constancy nourished his spirit.

A mountain, a desert, or a great forest might serve his need of strength, but water reflects his inner needs. Its all-enveloping quality, its complete diffusion into the surrounding environment, the fact it is never twice quite the same and each approach to it is a new adventure, give it a meaning all its own. Here a man can find himself and all his varied and changing moods. No wonder the Psalmist said:

He leadeth me beside still waters,
He restoreth my soul.

I have never forgotten my friend and our paddle in the dusk, and though he has been gone a long time, I still remember the light in his eyes when he turned to me from the bow of the canoe and said: "The witching hour."

I have cherished those hours, watched and waited for them no matter where I have been. I have known them many times on Listening Point and on distant waterways far beyond, have learned the signs and symbols that announce them. Sometimes they come without warning, mere flashes of the hours they might have been.

Just before dusk one day I stood at the end of the road looking up at the tall aspen, the spruces and balsams tucked among them, my mind full of what I had done. As I started up the narrow trail toward the cabin, I sensed the isolation that was there, but not until I reached the top of the hill and caught the first glimmer of the lake and its shine through the trees had I really arrived.

I walked to the end of the point and sat down. Long swells washed the rocks, and the chucklings that came from them soon were echoed within myself. As I looked and listened, all the confused hurrying of the day was slowed down and seemed to merge with the quiet movement of the water.

The colors deepened, reflections to the north and south became ragged silhouettes of black. In the center of the channel's iridescence was a spreading field of gold and apple green. Gradually the silhouettes began to close the gap between them, and suddenly the glory was gone. I sat there a long time and watched the black trunks of the pines against the burnished glow of the west. The calm of the lake and its beauty were now a part of me.

I went into the cabin, touched a match to the kindling in the fireplace, and the old jackpine logs of the interior became alight with the flames. Later, I lay watching the flickering shadows against the rafters, listened to the steady wash of the waves until the sound of them fused with my consciousness and I drifted off to sleep.

At dawn all movement was gone and there was only stillness. While there was a faint glow in the eastern sky, the shores were black. As I stood there waiting and listening, dawns of the past rushed back to me, smells and sounds and feelings I had known—the golden rice fields of Basswood Lake when islands rested like battleships in the mist; Lake Superior, when its fullness threatened to overflow its shores; Kashapiwi, when the waters trembled between the cliffs; and many more. Most vivid of all was the memory of a dawn on the Churchill River far to the north. Why, out of all that complex of half-forgotten memories, this one should stand out more boldly than the rest, I do not know, but in a flash I was standing on a great ledge close to a swirling pool.

The east was reddening, the falls above and the rapids below tinged with color, the air surcharged with the vast excitement of plunging water. How pungent the smell of the fire that morning, how sharp its crackling, how good the cup of coffee before its blaze. There was no thought then of the rapids we must shoot, the portages ahead, or the miles we might have to paddle on stormy lakes. In the aliveness and in the poetry of that breaking day, nothing seemed impossible. We were part of a great river flowing toward Hudson Bay, part of its beauty and at one with its surging power.

By midmorning, a spanking breeze brought out the white-caps. The sky was cloudless, the water blue, the air fresh and cool, a day for action and exploring. We launched the canoe, pointed its bow into the teeth of the wind, and fought the waves toward a point of land a mile away. Skirting the rocks with their spouting plumes, we landed in a protected little bay, climbed the slope to a level shelf among the Norways, and sat there on a bed of smooth pine needles watching the waves roll in and dash themselves against the ledge below.

Though marching combers might pin you down for hours, though you may be windbound on an exposed and rocky point for days at a time, if the sun is shining and your captors are blue and topped with silver spray it is no hardship, for the waters are full of song. When rapids glint and their shouting is glad and free, the treachery of hidden rocks and ledges is forgotten, and the canoe moves in and out with a sureness born of the lightness of spirit that comes from them. Running before a gale when spume is white and blowing in the wind and the water is in a sparkling champagne mood is no time for somber thoughts. On such days you can shout and sing to the wind, for witching hours are there for the taking. As I sat there beneath the pines, the magic of those days came back and the joy of glittering movement was in me.

But when there is no wind or the faintest intimation of a breeze and all the roughness of the water is erased, when reflections are so stark and clear it is hard to tell them from the shores, all thoughts of action disappear as well. Even so, there is witchery at work, though its magic is of a different kind. At such times it seems word has been passed that nothing should be done, and those who would move faster than in a dream do so at their peril. Paddling becomes difficult then, packs on portages double their weight, and everything is slowed to the pace the lake has set.

It was so on Mirond, its long unbroken reaches extending endlessly toward the south, and on the great Wollaston when mirages on the far horizons played tricks with eyes and one could not tell whether the shores were five or forty miles away. It has been that way on Sturgeon and Rainy and countless times on smaller lakes when canoes seem to be floating high above the water, and thoughts drift with them in an all-engulfing quiet that penetrates minds as well as bodies. There is no opposing such vast placidity, for like a cloud it flows around you. But if you allow yourself to become a part of its languor you may know the witchery of complete abandonment.

Calm may also mean the gathering of forces long held in leash. On one such day I came to the point when the lake was as still as it had ever been. Magnificent thunderheads piled high and moved across the sky, but there was no movement underneath. Not a leaf or a blade of grass stirred, and there was not a ripple on the surface of the water. A yellow light hung over all the land, and under its glow was uneasiness and fear. Everything was placed under cover, the canoes well back in the trees, firewood beneath the eaves, whatever could blow away made fast. Flashes of lightning came from the thunderheads and rolling peals of sound. Ducks flew madly past the point into the protection of the river mouth and then came back again. Birds dashed swiftly into cover and songs were hushed. A squirrel crouched quietly between a huge branch and the trunk of a pine, sat there cowed and waiting for the storm.

A slick smoother than the rest showed off the point and it was yellow with the light. A school of minnows skittered like bursting bubbles across its surface as a great pike rolled lazily where they had been. Loons ran across the water and their calling was wild and uncontrolled. Seagulls coasted far out from shore and for once their mewing was stilled.

Now it seemed quieter than before and an ominous sound of rushing came from everywhere at once. Trees swayed on top of the ridge and then along the shore; in a moment the lake was full of angry waves and they were crashing against the rocks. Thunder rolled, a bolt of lightning struck a pine on a far hilltop, and a dead aspen crashed to the ground near by. Norways swayed and bent as the earth beneath them lifted and trembled.

Then came the rain, and with it hail. The water was churned to froth, and the ground became white. I sat inside the cabin and watched the assault of the storm against the point, the pines and the tall and brittle aspen, looked out at the tossing combers and the spray as they hurled themselves against the ledges. The rain streamed off the eaves, then settled down to a slow and steady drumming; as I listened the wind died and the vast gray wetness of the lake absorbed all violence. Then it was over—only the dripping from the trees onto the sodden moss and brush.

I stepped outside to survey the damage. The ground was strewn with branches, the shoreline littered with needles and debris. Suddenly the sun burst out from behind a black scudding cloud and sprayed the shore with the glory of its light. Gulls flew high, silver breasts gleaming. Squirrels chattered, harvesting the cones that had fallen to the ground. A whitethroat sang, rather haltingly at first, grew brave, then whistled loud and clear.

A strange and complex witching hour, it had been a combination of many I had known, of twilight and dawn, of calm and violence, and even gaiety toward the end.

But of all the moods, all the variations of feeling and experience the waters of a lake can give, it is moonlight that is most remembered, for here is a strange excitement born of man's long and intimate involvement with its light. There is

mystery when paddling down the gleaming avenues between islands silhouetted against its glow, unreality in the
colonnades of tall trees or in the silvery reeds reflected in
the shallows. My memories are full of it—cypress swamps
in the south with their hanging festoons of Spanish moss,
little ponds gleaming like silver medallions in dark timber, the
full glory of an unbroken path of it down one of the great
waterways of the north, a castle moat in England shining like
polished pewter.

At Listening Point it seems best when watching the moonrise from the high rock, seeing its first glimmer over the
ridge and its slow majestic emergence, pulsating and trembling, until at last the huge orange ball is free of the horizons,
grows high and white to clothe the point and all the lake
with its enchantment.

These witching hours blend one into the other as calm may
blend into storm, for water reflects not only clouds and
trees and cliffs, but all the infinite variations of mind and
spirit we bring to it.

CHAPTER 6

CRADLE-KNOLLS

B ACK of the point are several pine stumps, their great buttresses evidence of size and age. They are covered with mosses and lichens, and in their cushioned softness grow dwarf dogwood, linnaea, and young balsams. Around one of them several maples have taken root and are now quite tall. Some of the older stumps are rounded mounds slowly sinking into the duff from which they came.

Princess pine twines around their bases, and the ground is green with tiny upright stems.

Among the stumps are cradle-knolls marking the windfalls long before the lumberjacks came through. Such knolls used to puzzle me until I walked through an old pine stand where a recent tornado had uprooted windrows of the great trees. There they lay, all pointing in the same direction, their roots sharp and ugly against the sky. When I found an old blowdown of a century before, where the fallen trees long ago had decayed, I knew the answer. On the windward side where the trees had been torn from the ground was a hollow, on the lee was a mound, with the trunk forming a straight low ridge in the exact direction of its fall.

Settlers in the pine country called these hollows cradle-knolls because the depressions on the windward side reminded them of old-fashioned cradles. I walked over to a cradle-knoll, kicked away the duff, and there within a few inches was subsoil and gravel. The mound showed deeper humus, for that was the forest floor before the blow. I followed the low ridge that led away from the mound, and there, as expected, was the reddish decay of the old trunk and a couple of sound pine knots that had defied a century of weathering and decay.

Here was a wind and tornado record for all time, a weather-vane of the past, as definite an indicator as the marks of glacial striation on the rocks of the point. The storm had come from the west, and each mound told a story of the ancient cycle of birth to old age.

I stood there beside three old stumps and the cradle-knolls and pictured what the forest had been like, the straight shafts unbroken by any disfigurement of branches except at their very tops, tall and proud and beautiful, the climax of development in the north country. On the ground then was little brush, no bushes or growth of any kind except in small areas where the sunlight filtered through. In such places were a few dwarf dogwood, some wintergreen, and the fragile stems of linnaea, with a cluster or two of fern. But mostly the ground was deep with needles, a layer of duff six inches or more in depth. Beneath that brown carpet was the black humus, the real wealth of the forest, the accumulated fertility of thousands of years.

That forest was mature and ripe, the final stage toward which all growth in the region trends. There are differences of opinion among ecologists and foresters as to what is the final growth or climax in this part of the north. Some say it is the balsam-spruce, others balsam and jackpine, some that it may even be a combination of balsam and hazel because these stands seem to last the longest, but I have always felt the climax should be interpreted as a matter of dominance, no matter how long it lasts. To me those great pines were the mature forest, evidence of their undisputed dominance over all other types. When they died, a train of events was set in motion, a succession of lesser trees which eventually prepared the way for them again, building up the microbiology of the soil, restoring to it the complex of biotic factors necessary for their eventual return. The pines could not grow

46

forever any more than the types that preceded them, and because of the almost impenetrable layer of needles beneath, there was little reproduction. The big trees took substances from the soil which could only be replenished by those coming in. They needed the aspen and the birch, the balsam and the spruce, and all the ground cover that went with them.

In a little valley just below were aspen, tall and straight, and on a slope beside them a growth of shining white birch, just beyond a stand of balsam and spruce, and through them all vigorous young pines thrusting upward toward the light, waiting for the time when the soil would be ready for them.

The aspen and birch would die well within a century; the tops of some already were beginning to wither. Then would go the balsam and spruce, and more and more pine would shoulder in. Eventually they would stand alone, thrive and grow tall in the fertile decay the others had provided. Everything was working toward the climax, striving toward the day when the great cycle would be repeated.

As I stood there in the soft September sunshine watching the leaves of aspen and maple drifting down over the old pine stumps and covering them with a variegated pattern of color, color they had never known during the centuries of their maturity, I saw the entire forest as a cycle of birth and youth, of middle and old age.

The birches and aspen growing below me in the valley are young, vivacious, and exuberant, in the very bloom of youth. In them is lightheartedness and movement, the thrill of constant change. No wisdom there, no maturity, for even though they may grow for fifty years or more they will still seem young. Among them is no feeling of the primeval, of great and hoary age, of stability and strength. Close to the end of their particular period there is about them a sense of impermanance, the sort of transient beauty which comes with flowers and herbaceous types that bloom and die each year.

In the stand of spruce and balsam there is a slowing down, a feeling of conservatism and middle age, a certain bowing to the inevitable completion of the forest cycle. Some of the spruce may last a hundred years or even more, but the balsam dies swiftly. Beneath them is the coming darkness, the preparation of the soil for a time when it will be in perennial shadow. Different lichens and mosses, bacteria and viruses and molds are now moving in to take the place of those which had grown there during the years when sunlight penetrated everything.

Not long ago, walking in a stand of climax pine, I was thinking of the meaning of those old trees with reference to those that had gone. Among them was no levity or laughter, but instead the somberness and gravity that goes with life that has been long and a goal attained. Looking up at the great black boles of the white pine and the reddish trunks of the Norways, listening to the soft whisper of the wind in the high branches, the nasal twang of the nuthatches among them, I sensed the benevolence that comes only with age.

Young before the American Revolution, these trees had

seen the voyageurs and were tall and straight long before discovery. Two to three hundred years of age, they now had reached the end of their growth. Someday in a wind they might sway and break, and going down they would be like ripe wheat before a scythe, falling one against the other, down in great windrows all pointing toward the east.

Or someday when the duff was tinder dry, a dead tree on some exposed ridge, poking its gray and pointed finger toward the sky, would reach for the lightning out of a black cloud, take it to itself, and begin to burn. Then the stub would crash to the ground in a cascade of sparks, and soon the entire forest would be aflame. The fire would race like a hurricane through the tops, and the great boles would fall crisscross and burn the soil to the rock. That would be the end, and for a few years the forest would be ugly and without growth, and rains and snows would wash the rocks until the whitened bones of them would show through the tangle of blackened debris that once were trees. Then slowly the green would come from underneath, the flowers and the fireweed and goldenrod. Seeds of aspen and birch would drift in and jackpine would spring from the tight little cones that somehow had survived the flames. Within a few years the new forest would come to life to cover the remains of the old climax stand.

For twenty-five years or more the woods would be a tangle of small brush, and deer would increase because of the browse. Birds would return and small mammals and insects, more life of all kinds than the forest had known for centuries. In fifty years the aspen and birch would be mature, and then the spruce and balsam would take over the land. A few old pines still standing after the fire would produce cones and scatter their seeds. Some would germinate, then the young pines would rear their tops once more and a new climax be in the making.

I looked at the cradle-knolls and the old stumps before me, at the fire scars deep within them, at the rotted hearts and the burrows of animals that for a long time had taken refuge there. Young pines of half a century and some now almost twice as old were everywhere. Out on the point the gnarled ones that gave such intriguing vistas were older, but even there were fire marks and the stumps of trees the loggers had cut. On the very end of the point the bearberry had taken root and the blueberry, and the ground was crimson with their color. That under-cover was as much a part of the climax stand as the trees themselves. Another century, barring the vagaries of fire, and the whole point area would go into the ancient climax again, and once more the wind would sigh in the tall tops and the ground be deep with duff.

I would not be there to see it, for the life of a man is short compared to that of pines, but I had been given a glimpse into the slow-moving cycles of growth and change. It was thrilling to be living in a period of movement and change, and I felt as much a part of it as the trees themselves. During my years on Listening Point, I could watch the inevitable march of species to fulfill their destiny, follow the steady succession of types one after the other in a pattern set by ages of adaptation. And while I would not see its completion, knowing the ancient stands of pine, I could see the climax forest as clearly as though the great trees were all around me.

CHAPTER 7

THE SOUND OF RAIN

L AST night in my tent I lis-
tened to the rain. At first it came down gently, then in a
steady drumming downpour, and I lay there wondering
when I would begin to feel the first rivulets creeping beneath
my sleeping-bag. The deluge continued, but there were no

exploring trickles, no mist through the roof of balloon silk. The tent, on the little rise with its thick cushion of bearberry, had perfect drainage all around, and the ropes were tied to two good trees. The gale could blow now and the rain come down, but I would be safe and dry the rest of the night. I settled down luxuriously to enjoy a sound I had known on countless campsites in the wilderness.

Like all woodsmen, I had planned for the morning, had tucked a roll of dry birchbark and a few slivers of pine under one end of the canoe. My packs were in one corner of the tent, the ax handy just in case something snapped during the night. The canoe was snubbed to a rock well up from the shore.

The wind came up and the tent swayed, but the ropes held; in the rain they grew taut as fiddle strings and the tent more waterproof with each new assault. A branch swished close and two trees rubbed against each other. The woods were full of sounds, creakings and groanings, with branches dropping from the trees.

How much good the rain would do, how fresh the water in every stream, how flowers would pop with the sun, the linnaea, the anemones, the dogwood and everything else along the trails. The ferns on the rocks would begin to grow again, and the silvery caribou moss would be soft and resilient with just a tinge of green. The dry and brittle lichens along the cliffs would turn from black to velvet green. Mushrooms and toadstools would suddenly emerge from every dead log, and the dusty humus would bring forth growths that had been waiting for this very hour, for no rain had fallen in a month.

The coming of the rain soothed a longing within me for moisture and lushness after the long-continued drought. As I lay there, I too seemed to expand and grow, became part of the lushness and the rain itself and of all the thirsty life about me. This is one of the reasons I like to hear the rain come down on a tent. I am close to it then, as close as one can be without actually being in it. I have slept in many primitive shelters, under overhanging cliffs, in lean-tos made of spruce boughs and birchbark, in little cabins roofed with poles and sod. I have slept under canoes and boats and under the spreading branches of pines and balsams, but none of these places gives me quite the feeling I get when sleeping in a tent.

The drops are muffled by the cloth, none of the staccato drumming there is under a hard roof. Once I slept in a cabin with a tin roof and listened to a chorus that night that was too violent to enjoy, a mechanical sound as though a thousand drums had broken into a rolling crescendo all at once.

Not long ago I met an old friend, C. K. Leith, one of the world's most famous geologists. He had been a professor of mine, and for a time I had worked under him on the Wisconsin Geological Survey. After his retirement, he had served as a consultant to the government, using his great knowledge of the world's minerals to guide exploration and development.

We sat in the Cosmos Club one rainy afternoon talking

about the old days, the days in the bush when he was a legend of endurance and fortitude, of the treks he had made into the far north that even today are contemplated with awe and wonderment by hardened prospectors. He was eighty-two when I talked to him last, but still as straight and energetic as ever. Suddenly he was quiet, a faraway look came into his eyes as he sat watching the rain spatter down into the courtyard.

"Do you know where I'd like to be right now?" he said finally. "In my old tent somewhere, safe and dry with nothing to do but listen to the rain come down."

He smiled and I knew he was cruising the back country of the Canadian Shield, down its brawling rivers, across its stormy lakes, knowing again the feeling of distance and space, the sense of the old wilderness.

"As you get older," he said, "and more involved with world affairs, you lose that life, but those were the good old days for me."

When I heard of his passing, I knew that somewhere back in the bush he was listening to the rain come down and that he had found again the life he loved.

In the woods of Listening Point, the drops soak into the ground as they should, stopped by an intricate baffle system of leaves and pine needles, small sticks and bits of bark, the partly decayed vegetation just underneath, and finally the humus itself, rich, black, and absorbent, the accumulation of ten thousand years. Here in the north it takes over a thousand years to form a single inch of it, and if the glacier receded from seven to ten thousand years ago, the humus on the point has taken just that long to form.

Below the humus is the mineral rock soil, the result not only of the grinding of glacial ice but the gradual breakdown of the granite and schist and greenstone by the frost and rain, the action of the acids of countless roots, the burrowing of hordes of insects and worms and beetles. This layer rests upon the native ledge, but by the time the rain reaches it, it has slowed and soaks into it without loss. There are no rivulets except where the rock is bare, no erosion or run-off to the lake. All that falls stays there and moves into the water table of the area to be held in reserve.

It was good to lie in the tent knowing the rain was replenishing the water supply, that none of it was being lost except where it ran off the smooth rocks, that even between them, in every cleft and crevice where there was any accumulation of humus at all, it would be held for months to come.

I awakened once during the night. The muffled drumming was gone and there was only a steady dripping from the trees, a sort of settling down and rearranging of the entire moisture pattern. I went to sleep almost immediately and didn't wake until dawn. The sun was shining then, and the little bay was heavy with mist. I stepped out of the tent and looked at a clean world. Every needle glistened, the rocks shone, all the debris of a month of dryness had disappeared. The point looked scrubbed and shiny too. I took my little roll of birchbark and the kindling and started the fire, made a cup of coffee and fried some bacon, but decided before I began any work I must walk down the trail to see what had happened along the shore.

The trail was lush and the needles beaten flat. Many leaves lay there, for in the wind and rain all those not strong enough in their holdfasts had fallen to the ground. Many little twigs and branches had been beaten off by the purging storm. Only the live wood had been strong enough to withstand it. Mushrooms and fungi were pushing through the humus, and one shaped like a whitened hand groped skyward with delicate fingers.

On a stump was a tiny patch of painted lichen, each silver tip brushed with carmine. A mossy log beside the trail now bloomed with linnaea, the tiny flowers bell-like twins, none of them over a quarter of an inch in length. There were literally hundreds of them covering the bright-green moss of the log. I knelt down, buried my face in them, and caught one of the subtlest odors in the north. Scientists call them linnaea for the famous Swedish botanist Linnaeus, who first named them in the north of Sweden. He loved the little flower, and it is significant of his feeling that the best-known painting of him shows one in his hand.

That patch of linnaea had a special significance after the rain, for it seemed to epitomize the resurgence of growth in all the area. The tiny flowers were part of June, part of early summer, and their odor presaged all the smells to come. This also was part of listening to the rain come down, for in the listening was the feeling that all life was responding to

the moisture, all forms benefiting and growing in the night.
I have always been fond of linnaea because it grows in the
shadows away from the direct glare of the sun, seems a part
of big timber and the depths of the wilderness, a spiritual
relative of the orchids that are also found there. How different from the harebells growing on the cliffs in the direct
sweep of the winds, flaunting their blue and wiry beauty to
space. They can stand the searing dryness of midday heat,
do not need the rains. The linnaean bells are shy and delicate,
would shrivel to nothing if protection were gone or the
rains did not come in time. As fragile as solitude, they would
disappear at the slightest intrusion.

Farther down the trail, in a patch of aspen and birch, I
found a late-blooming cluster of hepatica. Of a sudden I was
a boy again in the cut-over country of north Wisconsin
looking for the first flowers of spring. There the ground was
covered with them, while here they are rare. The rain had
brought out several blooms, the same sky-blue petals against
their sturdy clumps of fuzzy flattened leaves that I had
known years ago. I smelled the almost hidden fragrance of
the past, but more than the smell was the way those waxen
petals turned toward the sky. Someone told me long ago
they were bits of blue fallen to the earth, and to a child it
was the truth. No ordinary blue was this, but the kind one
sees in early morning after a rain and before the sun has
gained its brilliance.

On a little side-hill above the swale was a patch of dwarf
dogwood not yet in bloom. Soon the entire hillside would be

58

stippled with the four white notched petals typical of all the dogwoods on the continent, the great showy ones of the south whose drifts I had seen the spring before in the Blue Ridge country of Virginia. Up here only two or three inches in height, they make up for their lack of size as soon as the blossoms fade, for each produces a cluster of brilliant red berries that transforms the place of their growing from late summer until fall.

I had one more place to go, the swampy spot below the ridge. That was where a lady-slipper grew, so I left the trail and worked my way down into the boulders where open water now stood between the rocks. On a little shelf deep with a cushion of pine needles and well away from the dampness I found a single bloom, just as I had a year ago on the cliffs of Crooked Lake to the north. Down in the closed canyon of Crooked that day it was breathless and still. No wind stirred the water, and even the birds seemed weary with the heat. Wanting to get away from the closed-in feeling of the lake itself, I had climbed high onto the cliffs above the painted rocks.

On a great shelf carpeted with moss I rested, enjoying the panorama of wilderness far below me, the sweep of distant ridges with sky-blue waterways between them. Just then I happened to look down to the mossy shelf below and there in the shade made the discovery of the day, a single pink lady-slipper in full bloom. While I looked at it, I forgot the heat and humidity and thought of the great woods to the south where its closest of kin, the showy lady-slipper is found, and of all the great solitudes of the earth where members of the orchis family bloom. Alike in their needs, no matter where they grow, in the depths of tropical jungles or in the woods of the north, shadows and solitudes are part of their lives. They are flowers of the primeval and the unchanged places of the earth.

My lady-slipper just off the point was part of all that, as were the linnaea and the rest, part of the old wilderness I had known, part of the beating of rain on the tent the night before and of the lushness and fullness that had come with it.

CHAPTER 8

LAUGHING LOON

T HE canoe was drifting off
the islands, and the time had come for the calling, that moment of magic in the north when all is quiet and the water still iridescent with the fading glow of sunset. Even the shores seemed hushed and waiting for that first lone call, and when it came, a single long-drawn mournful note, the quiet was deeper than before.

Above came a swift whisper of wings, and as the loons saw us they called wildly in alarm, increased the speed of their flight, and took their laughing with them into the gathering dusk. Then came the answers we had been waiting for, and the shores echoed and re-echoed until they seemed to throb with the music. This was the symbol of the lake country, the sound that more than any other typifies the rocks and waters and forests of the wilderness.

To me only one other compares with it in beauty and meaning, the howling of the husky dogs around the Indian villages in the far north. Their wild and lonely music epitomizes the far reaches of the Canadian Shield, means nights when northern lights are a blazing curtain along the horizon.

While the northern loon in startling black and white, with its necklace of silver and jet and five-foot spread of wings, is of great interest scientifically, it is the calling that all remember. Whoever has heard it during spring and summer never forgets the wild laughing tremolo of the reverberating choruses.

One such night is burned into my memory. It was moonlight, the ice had just gone out, and the spring migration was in full swing. Loons were calling everywhere, not only on Knife but on adjacent lakes, and the night was full of their music from sunset until dawn. The echoes kept the calling going until it was impossible at times to tell which was real. While I listened it seemed to me that in that confused medley of sounds was a certain harmony as though major chords were being held for periods of time. It may have been imagination, but I have heard hints of it at other times as well. On this night there was no mistake, for the calling blended with the echoes until the illusion was complete.

The weirdest call of all is the yodel somewhat similar to the break in voice and the clear bugle-like note used by humans in calling across wide valleys in the Alps. This is the danger call used when a canoe is approaching a nesting area or when invasion is imminent. It can start all the loons within hearing, and when the yodeling blends with tremolo they are really making music.

The third call is the wail often mistaken for the howl of a wolf, and of much the same quality. It rises and falls in pitch and is used when a mate is calling for relief from its brooding on the nest or when signaling the young. Just that morning we heard it among the islands. We had been watching a pair swim slowly around the little bay where they had nested, with a lone chick riding sedately upon the back of one of them. When they saw us, they gave their warning calls at once, for that lone chick riding so grandly around the bay and no more than a day or two off the nest was far too small to fend for itself. We paddled toward them while the calling grew more and more intense, came at last directly between the parents and their young one, which now was trying desperately to dive. A week old it would have been able to submerge and swim for fifty feet or more, but this little chap was at our mercy and the parents were aware of its danger. At times they came almost within touching distance and tried to draw us away with the old ruse of pretending to have a broken wing and thus easy to catch. How they floundered and threw themselves about. When their enticements failed to work, they approached again, rearing up on their tails and uttering loud cries as they balanced there and all but treading water before flopping forward onto their breasts. The performance was repeated over and over again. They screamed and hooted and yodeled and gave the laughing call, but to no avail, while the chick, now confused and thoroughly frightened, swam hopelessly beside the canoe. Other loons in the vicinity swiftly joined the commotion, and the entire area was in turmoil.

Deciding they had been frightened too much, we turned and paddled back to the point, but for a long time after we had gone the calling continued. It was not surprising they were alarmed, for this lone chick brought out all of their protective instincts for the season of mating and nesting. Seldom owning more than two and often only one because of predation, they found in that last chick their whole excuse for being.

Just after the ice was out we had watched that pair come into the bay, stake out their nesting area, and repel invaders whenever they approached. One day we watched the courtship. They came toward each other slowly and, as they neared, dipped their bills rapidly in the water and just as rapidly flipped them out again. This was followed by several short swift dives, exaggerated rolling preens and stretchings such as only loons seem able to do. Suddenly they broke away from such intimacy, raced off across the water, striking the surface with powerful wing beats in a long curving path that eventually led back to where they had started. All during this time they indulged in the laughing call. Sometimes in the ecstasy of display they reared high on their tails as they did when their chick was endangered, struck their snowy breasts violently on the water, then raced again around the bay. Only once did we see this, but shortly afterward the mating was over and then we found the nest in a tussock of grass on a little swampy island close to shore and facing the open water. It was placed so they could slip off swiftly and reach the deeps should danger come behind them from the shore. The two olive-brown and somewhat speckled eggs were soon laid in a small shallow depression in the grass that was built up during the days of incubation until it was a concave little mound, each mate doing its share while it sat there, pecking and adding a grass blade at a time from the vegetation within reach.

A couple of weeks later one of the eggs was destroyed by some prowler, possibly a mink, a crow or a muskrat. The remaining egg now took all of their attention, and they guarded it jealously every moment of the day and night. If this had been stolen too, it would have meant a new nest and possibly another hatching.

Scientists say that in half the nests only one hatches out, and that the low rate of survival accounts for the fact that loons are never numerous. If two individuals reproduce themselves after their third year, then things are going well.

It is surprising in view of the high mortality rate that populations remain as steady as they do, that, in spite of predation, loons are found on almost every lake in the north.

One afternoon we sat on the point watching a flock of them playing on the open water. They had been there as a group since midsummer, bachelor loons and pairs that had not nested or had lost their eggs. Now free of responsibilities, these thwarted birds gathered each morning and spent the day together in the open. It may have been that the fishing was good in that particular spot, but I am tempted to believe they got together for a companionship that took the place of nests and young.

Suddenly one of the group called and then all together until the channel before us was again full of sound. Excited by their own music, they chased one another madly across the water, returning always to the place they had left. Toward dusk the flock began to disband, single birds first and then pairs flying back, no doubt, to their abandoned nesting areas. Sometime in the morning they would drift back again by ones and twos to spend the day together as they do on many of the larger lakes all summer long.

A pair flew close to the point and settled in the bay off the beach, and we watched them diving there for minnows, timing them to see how long they could stay submerged. Seldom did one stay under for more than half a minute, but there are records of dives as long as two and three minutes in duration. Some have been recorded even longer than that, but such observers may have failed to see a partial emergence for air. They are wonderful divers and swimmers, can pursue and overtake the swiftest of fish, and it has been said a loon can dive at the flash of a gun and be under water before the bullet strikes.

They can also submerge gradually, can control specific gravity possibly by a compression of feathers and expulsion of air from the lungs until the body is approximately the same weight as the water. All divers have a high tolerance for carbon dioxide, and oxygen needs are met, not from free air in the lungs, but from the oxyhemoglobin and oxymyoglobin stored in the muscles, substances responsible for the dark color of flesh in most waterfowl. This explains the diving, the gradual sinking from sight, and the fact that they have been caught on fishermen's set lines in Lake Superior at depths of two hundred feet.

Once I sat in a canoe at Lower Basswood Falls and watched a loon fishing in the rapids not fifty feet away. Suddenly the bird dove and swam directly under the canoe not two feet below the surface. The wings were held tightly at the sides and the legs the sole means of locomotion. When a young chick is learning to swim beneath the surface it uses both legs and wings, a reversion perhaps to the days of its reptilian ancestors; a habit generally abandoned, however, when it becomes adult.

It was now much too dark to see and we left our loons for the light and warmth of the cabin, but in the morning we watched them again. The pair had stayed close to the bay during the night and now were swimming around in the sunshine, getting ready to join the gathering flock on the open lake. We watched them, the brilliant black-and-white markings on their backs, saw one preen, rolling over on its side exposing the silvery-white breast until it glittered and shone in the morning sun. The other rose to its full height, flapped its wings vigorously, and settled down again. Then both dove with scarcely a ripple to mark their descent and soon were far past the point, heading for the rendezvous.

Some say that loons eat too many fish and should be reduced in numbers, but as the population on most lakes is small, with usually only one or two per square mile of the area, this is a ridiculous assumption. To be sure, they do eat fish, but, like most predators of the type, they also eat insects, mollusks, crustacea, and even vegetation. We can well afford to keep them, for their aesthetic value far outweighs any other consideration. Without the music of their calling and the sight of them on the open water, the lakes of the north would never be the same.

A pair flew overhead, and we heard plainly the whistle of their wings, watched the slow and powerful beats as they headed across the lake. As they passed the gathering flock they gave the tremolo once and then settled down with the rest. I had hoped they might do what I had seen them do in the past, glide into the waiting group with wings set and held in a motionless V above their backs. Once I had seen them come in that way on Kekekabic, approaching the lake like seaplanes about to land in a long unbroken glide from the top of the ridge to the water's surface.

68

But, while they are strong flyers and can swim and dive as few birds can, they are absolutely helpless on land, and only once have I seen one more than twenty feet from water. I was coming across a portage with a canoe on my back, and there, to my amazement, was a loon standing bolt upright in the center of the trail. I was so startled by the apparition in black and white that its scream of alarm almost made me drop the canoe. The bird turned and literally hurled itself toward the shore, half flying, swimming and running on its ridiculously tiny legs. With a wild water-choked yelp it plunged into the shallows and out to diving depth and swiftly disappeared. That explained why nests are always close to the shore. Loons must be able to slide instantly into the water, cannot waste precious moments struggling over land. No creature is clumsier out of its element than this great diver of the north.

The sound of a whippoorwill means an orange moon coming up in the deep south; the warbling of meadowlarks the wide expanses of open prairies with the morning dew still upon them; the liquid notes of a robin before a rain the middle west and east; the screaming of Arctic terns the marshes of the far north. But when I hear the wild rollicking laughter of a loon, no matter where I happen to be, it means only one place in the world to me—the wilderness lake country and Listening Point.

CHAPTER 9

YOUNG OTTERTAIL

As I sat on the end of the point watching the sunset and looking toward the west and the wild country of Lac la Croix, a day's paddle beyond, I thought of the legend of young Ottertail. Why I thought of him just then I do not know except that the moment was one of mystery and my mind ranged to far places that spoke to me of mood. Such a place was Pine Point on Pickerel Lake to the north on the Canadian side, the burial place of a young Indian of the Lac la Croix band.

One moonlit night I was camped there, and it was then I heard the story of how long ago an Ottertail of the Chippewas had carried the body of his son through miles of wilderness and laid him to rest in the most beautiful spot he knew. There among towering red pines he buried the youth who would have been the poet of his tribe, the boy who someday would have put into song the longings and legends of his people.

When death swooped down on the Indian village at the mouth of the Snake River and took him away, the father knew he must find a spot where the spirit would be at peace and, because the boy loved great trees and a song was always in his heart, chose the cathedral pines on Pickerel Lake.

Two days by canoe from the village, he laid the body to rest in a shallow grave at the very end of a tremendous colonnade of Norway pines. Over the grave he built the traditional shelter of bark and cedar, leaving an opening at one end so the spirit could come and go at will.

Legend has it that on nights when the moon is full and birds are wakeful with its light, the spirit of young Ottertail leaves its resting-place and walks among the pines down to the sand beach on the west shore of Pickerel Point. There it stands and gazes toward the village of Lac la Croix.

When the waters are still and the moonlight more than beautiful, the spirit may even leave the point, drift across miies of wilderness toward the home it once knew. It was seen watching for sturgeon below the first falls of the Snake, and another time a phantom canoe moved among the calling loons of Lac la Croix, a canoe that never left the loons and never came to land, just drifted there and then, like a morning mist, faded from view.

Just before dawn it was seen floating like a wraith along the edges of muskegs where they came close to the water. There are some who have seen it in the rice beds in September, a lone canoe always at dusk or at dawn, with the rice sticks beating rhythmically and the canoe moving through the rows of bundled stalks, clear to the end of the ricefield and back again, when all the other canoes were at the parching or in the woods hunting and no new people had come in.

There are some who swear they have seen it on the portages where the rivers come close to the trails, for all of these places young Ottertail loved. With the coming of dawn, the spirit is always back at Pine Point, and there it rests until the coming of the next full moon.

As I sat there watching the burnished gold of the horizon change to mauve and blend with the water, I wondered if the spirit were again on its way. The moon had risen behind me, and even before the color was gone from the west it was silvering a path through the iridescence of the afterglow. On such a night his spirit might be stalking through the checkerboard of gloom beneath the pines or standing on the beach looking back toward the Indian village.

It might be moving up the Indian Sioux out of La Croix into the Vermillion; then, floating over the lake, it might descend the Tamarack as Indians had always done to the mouth of the river not two miles off the point. The spirit land of the Chippewa, the spirit lands of all peoples, how important to catch their meaning, how little we know when we see only rocks and trees and waters, mountains and meadows and prairies, how impossible to catch the feeling of any country without sensing its legendry and the mystery of what cannot be seen, places that always speak of the unknown.

There are many places close to the point that have this feeling of mystery; one is Darkey Lake, which Indians never cross without hushing their voices. Darkey is far more than a good trout lake, more than a link in the route to Brent and the country to the east, far more than the outlet of the Minn River to Martin's Bay of Lac la Croix. These are part of the physical terrain that all travelers know, but the mood and feeling of the lake, the knowledge that here the spirits dwell, give it poetry.

Not long ago I passed that way. The day was glowering, the wind holding out of the southwest. We fought our way from the eastern entrance through the whitecaps, down to the cliffs with the pictured rocks, sat below them in the lee and studied the great serpent of the horned head with the canoes paddling beside it, the moose showing the tracks of hunters on either side, the lichen-covered figures no longer plain enough to understand. As we sat there under the wild scudding clouds and their spattering of sleet, I could not help but feel that ghostlike canoes were there beside us.

The Kawishiwi country of "no place between" is another such area just to the east of the point, a no-man's-land of the past, a portion of the spirit world that was once part of the lives of Indian tribes long gone.

The upper reaches of Kawnippi also speak of unknown things. On Massacre Island, at the mouth of the Wawawiaga-mak, a battle took place many years ago. Old guns have been found there, baskets for the making of maple sugar and the remains of an old encampment. I never slip into the river's mouth without being conscious of the past, without wondering what happened there.

But mystery drawn from personal associations may be as powerful as that of long ago, the feeling that in certain places old friends are still alive and happenings in your own life are as vivid as before. Such a place is the mouth of the Range River where it empties into Low Lake on the route from Burntside to Jackfish Bay of Basswood Lake. With a friend now long gone I spent many happy days there, and when I stop at the campsite we used, I find things still unchanged. There in a cleft between the rocks was where we stored our extra food and cooking outfit, there the grassy shelf where we rolled our bags when the weather was good and the sheltered spot in the jackpines when gales blew out of the north. Not long ago on a night when the snow was spitting and ice forming in the shallows, I was there alone, but the past was with me and my friend was young and full of laughter and we were gay as we listened to the storm.

There are many places that even without legendry or personal associations speak of mystery. Such a spot is a broad shelf of rock just back of the point, a little glade tucked into the woods away from the lake. No trees are there, but over the rocks is a thick carpet of caribou moss and blueberry. I sat there in the moonlight not long ago and it seemed as though all the voices of the woods spoke to me, as they always do in glades wherever they might be. There is something about a glade when the moonlight filters in and trees are black against the sky and you have the sense of being in a great room that speaks of unseen things. A horned owl hooted while I was there and birds chirped sleepily, and as I listened it became a place of magic and the world was far removed. In such a place the wilderness holds meanings far beyond what it has in the light of day. There young Ottertail might have stood looking toward the Indian village at the mouth of the Snake on Lac la Croix.

Another place just south of the beach is where huge boulders stand among the pines. In among them is a powerful sense of the primeval, and those enormous blocks of stone make me feel as though great forces are all about me, that I can feel the moving of the ice sheet that dropped them there ten thousand years ago. So I felt at Stonehenge one night in England, and in the Druid circles on the high downs where men of the past had communed with the unknown.

W. H. Hudson, in speaking of his boyhood on the pampas,

said it well: "I used to steal out of the house alone when the moon was at its full to stand silent and motionless near some groups of large trees gazing at the dusky green foliage silvered by the beams, and at such times the sense of mystery would grow until a sensation of delight would change to fear and the fear increase until it was no longer to be bourne."

There are many places that have mood whether the moonlight shines or not, though in its light it may be easier to catch than in the light of day—places that, because of a combination of physical circumstances, have a character all their own. I think of Glacier Lake up the Fauquier chain from Louiza to the Saganagons River, the campsite at the far east end from which you can look down its full length to the portage in the west. Somehow Glacier, with its high, almost mountainous shores, gives one a sense of space and removal, a feeling of unlimited distance and the unexplored. Though an old canoe route traveled by many, it has never lost its character. Standing there at dusk and looking down that long mysterious expanse, I feel it must go on and on, that beyond it are places men have never been.

On the way to Glacier Lake between Burke and Sunday is a shallow stream known as Singing Creek. This outlet of Sunday Lake ripples over stones, is shaded with cedar, and from the campsite beside it is a vista of the waterway above. I never camp there without being a part of its music. Here laughter comes easily and there is no sense of the primeval or the unknown. This is a place for banter and fun, and songs are as natural as those that come from Singing Creek itself.

To lie there at night and listen to the chuckling of the water means happy dreams. There is no somberness here, no mysterious sense of the past, but poetry there is and a mood that sings.

The sun was down and the moon high, the night growing chill. The point was part of the legendry of the north and all its moods. In time it would grow into all the places I had known and build for me a legendry of its own. What mood it would have in the years to come depended on what happened there and the joys and sorrows that would weave themselves into its rocks and trees and vistas and be as much a part of it as they.

CHAPTER 10

WILDERNESS BEACH

THE wind had held from the
southwest for several days and the little strip of beach across
the channel was clean as a sheet of paper, ripple marks
showing far into the shallows. The water was quiet now, but
a thin line of pine needles moved slowly back and forth in

the long and easy swell. It was as though the lake still felt the waves, remembering their thunder.

A lone sandpiper ran down the fresh surface of the sand, leaving a row of tiny tracks. It stopped at the end of the beach and teetered back and forth like a little boy wondering if it were quite safe to rush in. Like all the sandpipers in the world, along the beaches of the wilds, the oceans, even the crowded ones near towns and cities, this one followed the ebb and flow, its tiny legs twinkling as it danced back and forth watching for bits of food washed shoreward by the surge.

But others had written on the beach as well. A field mouse had strayed from the sedges, taken a swift exploring run, then, frightened by the movement of the water, had leaped for the protection of its jungle of stems. A red squirrel had also investigated the smooth surface at the base of a spruce and then had scurried high into its cone-laden top. Even a mink had approached from the water, run its entire length, and returned to the far end. Clean sand—what strange fascination beckoned creatures of the wild?

Newspapers of the forest, I had read them often in the past, on the big beach of Lake Insula with its broad sweep below the pines, on Lac la Croix where the ranger station stands. on the sand spit of Ile à la Crosse on the route to Athabasca and the Mackenzie, on countless little beaches such as this, strips of white or golden sand tucked into forgotten bays as temporary records of the wilds. I had read the great ones too, Daytona with its white sands brought

79

down the coast from the Appalachians and dropped along the Florida shore, the black beaches of the Mediterranean where volcanic sands glittered against indigo blue, the golden beaches of the far north tracked only by moose and caribou.

But the little ones I enjoyed the most, for theirs is an intimacy of language I can understand; no glaring headlines or sensational stories, simply a quiet account of those who had passed. There is such a little beach on Robinson Lake just north of the border, the sand there white as the one off the point, with ripple marks even farther into the shallows. Facing the north on an island, it is warm only at noon, for only then is the sun high enough to shine upon it. No large animals ever walk there, only gulls and sandpipers, mice and squirrels, but from it I can see the narrows and the islands with their wind-blown pines and on moonlight nights can look into the reaches beyond and feel that I am part of all the beauty and mystery it commands. There I have the same sense of closeness and understanding that comes with a personal note. Such little beaches are more than newspapers, rather private affairs with much between the lines.

All beaches have similar origins, from the flooded one in the arm of Listening Point to the great scimitars of the oceans, inevitably the result of erosion of coasts or mountains and the deposition of rubble and talus where waters can grind them to sand and carry them to some final resting-place.

Waves are powerful agents of erosion and exert tremendous pressures against the land. Over the deeps they roll forward with an oscillating movement, but approaching shore they drag the bottom, losing freedom and speed as they become burdened with sediment. It is then they really show their white-capped plumes; hurling themselves against the cliffs into crevices, caves and hollows, they act as giant hammers and wedges of destruction. Falling back, they create vacuums that break the surfaces and rend them apart. Here are the blowing holes, the spouting rocks, the thunder and roar of rocky coasts as the waves gather their plunder and race back with it toward the deeps from which they came.

Once over the Pacific I watched a storm beating the great beaches there, could all but hear the roar above the drone of the plane, saw the moving mountains of water from the west hurling themselves against the black shores and the yellow sands below. There in serrated rows as far as I could see were the beachmakers in action, using their tools of dislodged materials, sands and gravels, pebbles and even boulders, to carry on their endless task.

No matter what its hardness, the angular character of rock fragments is changed to the smoothly rounded form characteristic of coastal debris everywhere, and in time even the largest are reduced to sand and silt. The finer materials are carried out by the undertow, the coarser left near shore and a covering laid on lake or ocean floor extending from the deeps landward to the limit reached by the highest waves. Over this covering, which in time produces the beach, rages a contest between the surface waves and their returning undertow. If the waves win and carry more to the shore than is brought back, the formation is assured. If the approach is steep, the undertow may win for a time, but the battle is usually a losing one, for slopes become more gradual as erosion of the shore continues and more sediments are left behind.

Where waves strike the shore obliquely, the run of water generates a paralleling current which sweeps along the coast carrying its burden until it is slowed by some opposing flow, great and quiet depths, or an obstruction of the land mass itself. Only moving water can carry a load. When it is stopped, the sediment it carries is deposited. Beaches, spits, and sandbars result wherever this takes place, just as they are formed where rivers meet deep water at their mouths. So were formed the sand spit of Minnesota Point where the St. Louis empties into Lake Superior, and bars at the mouths of countless streams wherever their turbulent waters are stilled.

The formation of the little beach before me was no different from all the rest. Its basic materials came from the erosion of the Laurentian Mountains millions of years ago, sands and gravels that were deposited in ancient river beds and valleys. When glaciers came, gouging out the present lake beds, grinding what was left of the old ranges even more, polishing the surfaces they overrode, their roaring streams tumbling boulders in their beds and carrying all before them, the stage was set for the beaches of the north. Waves moved the sands about, washed and cleaned them, and spread them over the lake bottoms. Uncounted billions of them moved the sands toward this bay and many others. Uncounted billions of following undertows brought them back again, rolling granules against granules until they were worn almost to the fineness of dust and all but the resistant white quartz from the original granites had disappeared. In time the residue was destined to become even finer, and eventually it might be hard to distinguish one particle from the other. The fine ripple marks, the hard surface of this strip of sand, its gradual descent into the deeps indicated age and maturity of terrain with the task for the era almost completed.

Though this bit of beach was barely a stone's throw in length, from it I could see all the beaches in the world, but this one had a distinction for me that many others could not boast, for it had not changed perceptibly since it was formed, was the same little strip of wilderness sand it had always been. No foreign debris had ever defiled it, no marks upon its surface except the stories of creatures who had enjoyed it just as I enjoyed it now.

While undoubtedly all beaches play an important part as feeding-areas due to their relative safety and the fact that many forms of aquatic life thrive and multiply there, they may mean more than that. Once I saw a bear with her cubs wading out to a sand spit, saw them stop at its end and gallop back and forth through the shallows with the spray flying high. On a sparkling summer morning a doe and twin fawns raced down the length of a long beach and then back again. They could have run on the sand, but preferred to run in the water. Last summer I saw a timber wolf trotting sedately across an open dune above the water, and time without number rabbits, squirrels and birds, not feeding but seeming to enjoy the peculiar delight that beaches provide. I cannot speak for them, but is it wrong to believe that they may know something akin to the lift of spirit that is mine when standing on the sands? Is there any reason they too should not have somewhat the feeling I do there of coming suddenly out of the mountains into an alpine meadow, or a clearing in dense woods, or a plain after traversing rugged broken country?

They seem to like swimming on a beach just as I do. The water, to be sure, is no different from water anywhere else, but perhaps they have the same sense of security there as I. Floating in the shallows, knowing one can touch a smooth hard bottom any time one wishes, means something to even experienced swimmers, for most forms of terrestrial life have never quite escaped the inborn fear of deep water.

One night not long ago when the little bay off the point was silvered with light, I lay there and floated over the sands knowing that even then the waves were rolling them slowly back and forth as they had in ages past. I swam down the path of the moon toward the rocky end of the point, turned and swam back again. How good to feel the sand at last, to drift there part of the moonlight and the beach and the long centuries that had gone into its making.

A hundred years ago great pines and cedars rimmed the

84

bay and the crash of combers during storms and the whispering of its sands when they were through were part of the music of Listening Point. In those days before the building of the logging dam at the outlet, the beach's smooth half-moon was well out of the water, but when the pines were cut and the level of the lake raised to drive them down the river to the mills below, the little beach was flooded. In time it may emerge again, but I can see where it begins a dozen feet off the rocks and the ripple marks running out as they have always done. In this tiny shelf of sand just off the shore is part of the story of the north, part of the story of all the beaches I have ever known. While no writing is done upon it now, the day may come when sandpipers will once more dance before its ebb and flow.

CHAPTER I I

FLEUR-DE-LIS

W E DECIDED to plant the fleur-de-lis next to the beach in a sheltered place between the rocks where the roots would be close to water and black humus that had washed between them would always be damp. A cluster of native blue iris grew near by whose roots I knew demanded identical conditions for survival. This was

86

no ordinary transplanting. The fleur-de-lis was a symbol of empire, the ensign of the kings of France, had been followed by brave men for many centuries.

The digging was difficult and many stones had to be moved before the acid soil was deep enough for the three little plants we had brought. When they were firmly set, we looked at our work with pride. The long green blades, though bruised by having been carried in a pack, pointed bravely to the sky. Now, when spring came, there might be gold as well as blue along the beach.

The fleur-de-lis, according to the historian Grace Lee Nute, is a native of Asia, was brought to Europe from the east by traders in silk and spice. So highly prized and significant did it become, so much beloved for its beauty and golden color, it was inevitable that feudal lords should adopt it as their emblem. When the new world was discovered and its exploration began, it was the golden fleur-de-lis that blazed the trails of the north.

It is no wonder that the early French colonists brought the plants along to remind them of the land they had left. What is more, the seeds when pulverized made a nourishing drink and the bulbs may have had some medicinal value. Whatever the reason, some of them found places where they could grow and have survived for nearly three hundred years since their arrival on the North American continent. In 1679 Daniel Greysolon, Sieur Duluth, a young nobleman of France, explored as far west as "fond du lac Superieur" the farthest end of the inland sea. Here, says Dr. Nute, a post was established. "Over it must have floated the king's ensign, which Duluth had carried so often in France, a white field studded with the conventionalized fleur-de-lis in gold."

Fond du Lac post, as it was called, was near the mouth of the St. Louis River where it empties into the bay. Two cities now lie on either side of the river, Superior on the south and Duluth on the north. We saw the plants while driving along the lake shore between the two ports. After crossing the bridge, the highway parallels the water and slips and estuaries that have been built for the boats. Just off one of them is a railroad embankment leading to the docks, not too far from the old fort. It was there we saw the fringe of gold, an unbroken line of it along the west side of the embankment. It was as though someone had brushed a yellow line between the blue of the water and the brown earth of the fill. We stopped and looked and were amazed. What golden plant could have found a foothold in such an unpromising place? We worked our way across a swamp to where they grew, and there they were, a fringe of iris, but unlike any we had ever seen. It was the golden iris of Europe, the famed fleur-de-lis of France.

The plants had found the environment they needed, would grow there forever if nothing interfered. But, aware that the St. Lawrence Seaway now under construction would mean deep dredging for ocean-going vessels, dredging that might mean their doom, we dug up three of the plants and brought them with us a hundred miles to the north.

We planted them first in a little marsh, but there was not enough sun and, though they bloomed, we could see they would not thrive. When we acquired Listening Point we decided to plant them near the beach where the native iris had already taken hold. There nothing would disturb them and they could grow until the end of time, reminding us of the voyageurs and the glory that was theirs.

It would be a fitting place for the fleur-de-lis, for this was a route of the early traders in fur and no doubt many times in the past they had stopped there to rest after the arduous trek from Fond du Lac to Lake Vermillion and Basswood some twenty miles to the east. The Quetico-Superior country knew them well, these adventurers from the towns of Montreal and Quebec who paddled their canoes not only the two thousand miles to the great trading post of Grand Portage on Lake Superior, but continued for three thousand more until they reached the Mackenzie, the Athabasca, Great Slave, and Great Bear next to the Arctic Ocean. This was part of the voyageurs' highway to the far northwest.

The diary of Alexander Mackenzie tells of a trading post near Prairie Portage on Basswood Lake, a post like the one at Fond du Lac of the Northwest Company. I visited that site not long ago, and as we fought the waves across Inlet Bay, I thought of the voyageurs who had come that way and how welcome a sight that post must have been to bush-weary travelers of the past. What a thrill for them to see the beached canoes and the flag flying over the fort, and how they sang as they thought of friends and warmth and rest. That trading post had been a landmark in the lives of many men.

We went ashore and explored the site, but all we could see was the line of demarkation where the timber stopped, where the pines had been cut to make room for the buildings that had stood there. Now the site was grown thickly with hazel and maple, poplar and birch, alder and diamond willow, and we had to hunt to find the telltale mounds and outlines of the foundations. We cut some stakes and began to dig in a corner of one of the buildings and there made our first discoveries, square-headed nails fashioned at forges almost two hundred years ago, bits of clay mortar, bones of deer and moose, turtles and fish, a flint skin-scraper and a pipe-stem—enough to know that men had lived there many years.

That night we camped on the smooth rocky shelf where birchbark canoes must have landed, and from there we could look over the expanse of Bailey Bay. The wind was blowing harder than ever and rows of whitecaps marched upon us out of the northwest. In front was a small, heavily timbered island which as yet had not known the logger's ax. That island looked then as it looked to us, and the men who sat before other campfires must have watched the breakers crashing around it and the last rays of the sunset turning those tall pines to gold. Men of those days dreamed of empires, lands to be explored and conquered.

We pitched our tent above the landing and below the site of the fort itself, and, lying there in our sleeping-bags listen-

ing to the wind whipping through the trees, it was not hard
to imagine it was a year in the seventeen hundreds, that on
the morrow we would continue our voyage toward the
uncharted expanses of the northwest.

But as important as the empire they dreamed of were
the gay, indomitable *voyageurs* who loved the wilderness
more than life itself, who could subsist on a pound of corn
a day, whose normal sleep after backbreaking toil was a
scant three or four hours, who could paddle and portage
sixty miles without rest, face the dangers of rapids and falls
and stormy lakes with no shelter from insects or the weather,
without question the hardiest and most adventurous travelers
of the bush the continent has ever known.

Legend is full of their exploits, and strange stories have
come down of the feats that they performed. The nine-mile
trail around the rapids of the Pigeon north of Lake Superior
was their proving-ground, and here they showed their
mettle. On the Grand Portage they packed their normal
load of two ninety-pound packets of fur or trade goods the
full nine miles; here too was where Jean Le Bolier packed
five such packets on a wager and won.

But the spirit of those men and their songs were even
more impressive than their feats of strength and endurance.
Those songs have come down to us, the gay lilting melodies
of *"En roulant ma boule"* and *"A la claire fontaine"* and
many others, for they sang as they paddled and the value of
a voyageur was based as much on his ability to sing the chan-
sons of Old France as on his strength.

91

The lakes running along the international border between Canada and the United States were once their major route of travel, for here came all the expeditions into the northwest. Through this waterway and its tributaries was funneled all the fur from the Saskatchewan and the Athabasca country and beyond. So well known was this section of the famous route that it was seldom neglected in diaries or reports. The portages then were possibly in better condition than now and the volume of traffic fully as great. Through here came Radisson and Groseilliers in 1660, La Vérendrye in 1731, Alexander Mackenzie in 1780, the Frobishers, Peter Pond, and all the rest. They knew the country well and left their names wherever they went, names with the sound of the wilderness—Lac la Croix, Dieu Rivier, and Grand Marais—reminders of the romantic days of the trade.

Just north of the point is a little island known as Blueberry. In the early days, so say those who know, the traders met the Indians there to carry on their transactions. It was always a time when the blueberries were ripe, and for a reason. A keg was filled with berries and rum was poured over them until it reached the top, making in time a purple punch of no mean strength. Not until the drink was finished did the trading begin, and fabulous deals were made under its influence.

And now along the little beach below the stark outline of the old point that they had known will bloom a patch of golden fleur-de-lis, a reminder of the days when the voyageurs came up from Fond du Lac on their way to the trading post on Basswood Lake. Who could have dreamed that someone a century or two hence would plant a few of their flowers of gold somewhere along the route in the far interior? Now when the iris blooms it will serve as a living symbol of an era when songs of the voyageurs floated among the islands, when feats of daring were commonplace along the wilderness roads they traveled. No one would have dared to say that sometime civilization would reach the far off *"pays d'en haut."*

The point has changed little since those early days, and the silhouettes of the islands and the vistas across the water are much the same as they have always been. I can sit here and dream of the past, for in the fleur-de-lis is a living bridge between the voyageurs and me.

During the day I had seen a canoe party start out for the Crab Lake portage at the west end of the lake, two boys stripped to the waist and bronzed as Indians starting out on a ten-day cruise to the border. They would follow the ancient portages between the lakes and around the rapids, camp on the same campsites the voyageurs once used. Though they might sing different songs, they would live in the tradition of bush travelers of the past and be free to follow any waterways they chose. They would know the same sparkling waters in the mornings, their opalescence at dusk, and the joy of new adventures no matter where they went. Though they would not pack the loads nor face the hardships, and would live in comfort the voyageurs never dreamed possible, they too would know the lure of the beyond.

93

For here the ancient highway is still unchanged, and to voyageurs for years to come its sights and sounds and smells will be the same as they always have been. They will pass the point on their way to the east and west and north, and the fleur-de-lis will watch them go and nod them on their way.

CHAPTER 12

BROAD-WING

I WAS brushing out the trail from the road to the beach, had come over the high rocky ridge and down the slope through a dense growth of pines and balsams close to the shore. It was raining gently, and each time I touched a tree I was showered with drops. A hundred yards from the water's edge where I could see through the wetness to the misty gray of the lake, I heard a strange sound. It seemed to come from a thicket to the right of the trail, the sort of plaintive hissing young animals sometimes make when frightened or alone. Quietly I threaded my way through the dripping underbrush toward where it seemed to be, but when I reached the thicket it came from somewhere else. Each time I tried to trace the sound, the same thing happened, with the calling as elusive as before.

I stood very still, did not move for several minutes, scanned every possible hiding-place beneath the trees, but all I could see were windfalls, damp pine needles, and sodden leaves.

Completely baffled, I worked my way back to the trail and stood beneath a scrubby white pine for protection. While listening to the hissing plaintive note and wondering where it actually might be, I noticed white calcareous droppings on the ground around me, and then I knew at once. Cautiously I looked upward and there, just as I had suspected, in a crotch about thirty feet overhead was a dark mass of sticks and looking over the edge of the nest were three scrawny young creatures with huge burning eyes watching my every move. Speckled a dirty grayish white, soaked by the rain, unkempt and disheveled, with sharply beaked faces, they looked like wizened little old men waiting for the end.

Amused and delighted by the caricatures they made, their complete immobility and absorption with the threat below them, I knew now I would not have long to wait before the mystery would be solved. Not a sound came from them, but off in the woods, constantly changing position, was the whistling I had heard before, a sound that was something like that of a wood pewee with more of a lisp perhaps: *tsve—whee—eeee, tsve—whee—eeee,* the unmistakable call of a broad-wing hawk. Not once did I see the bird, though I knew it was near, and then I remembered the power of ventriloquism that is theirs. Perched somewhere near by and possibly not moving at all, it would not emerge until I had gone.

The nest was built in the bushy top of the tree where sometime in the past the terminal shoot had been killed either by disease, insects, or a porcupine, resulting in the perfect shelter and support of a four-stemmed cluster of branches. On the point itself and also back along the ridge I had noticed similarly disfigured trees, each with an old abandoned nest, and no doubt there were others as well. Broad-wings had used Listening Point as a nesting-area many years before I came.

The young were two-thirds grown and would stay in the nest another month or six weeks before they were ready to leave. Not once had they moved a muscle, their spectral eyes as immovable as their bodies, while from all around came the warning call telling them to be still while I was near. Satisfied now, I left them and continued cutting the trail out to the beach.

The next day the sun came out, the skies were blue and the woods full of bird song and warmth. I had no sooner picked a good vantage point on a boulder down at the beach than a broad-wing sailed over me with barely a movement of wing tips, circled and circled along the shore, then settled down on a weathered stump with wings outspread as though still in flight. Balancing and weaving gently on its perch, it was watching for a mouse, a chipmunk, or perhaps a frog. Even a snake, a large beetle, or a salamander would do, anything big enough to carry but not so large as to be difficult.

Once it took to the air and I saw the white underwings with their black tips, the black bars beneath the tail. Then settling down again, wings fanning softly as before, it dropped suddenly to the ground and just as swiftly took to the air again with a field mouse clutched tightly in its talons. A slow flapping circle over the clump of pines and balsams and it was back at the nest and I knew the hungry three were tearing the mouse to bits.

Not a beautiful bird as hawks go, with none of the dash and color and arrogance of Cooper's hawk, the sharp-shin, or even the tiny sparrow hawk, it was brown and roughly speckled with no distinctive marks, a bird about the size of a crow with rather stubby wings and tail. One of the buzzard hawks, it is the least important of a rather commonplace group. Compared to the falcon hawks with their savagery, speed, and courage, the rakish beauty and domineering expression of those pirates of the skies, the broad-wing has never excited the admiration of men. Small, unglamorous and seldom seen except when the great flocks are moving in the spring and fall, they live their quiet uneventful lives alone in the deep recesses of woods, swamps, and waterways.

Seldom seen over fields or open clearings, the broad-wing enjoys solitude and the silences, belongs truly to the wilderness and its innermost sanctuaries, the quiet glades, the little pools and unknown creeks and rivulets that most travelers never see.

Only twice during the year do they emerge from their hiding-places. They gather in huge flocks while migrating in the spring and fall and give the impression of being far more numerous than any other species. There are many records from all over the country of such gatherings. On September 24, 1924, six or seven thousand were seen near Minneapolis, and at Wheaton, Minnesota, the following year fifteen hundred were shot during a single day. At famous Hawk Mountain in Pennsylvania, Maurice Broun recorded 11,392 on September 16, 1948. Even today at the traditional crossing-places of the continent thousands may be seen, especially in the fall, riding the cold northwest winds toward the south. While other hawks usually move in small groups, the broad-wings make a festival of migration, forget during the wild free days of travel that they are creatures of solitude and quiet, and demonstrate to the world that they too are hawks and that deep within them are hidden qualities of all the breed.

The very fact of their gathering in enormous flocks leads to the impression that they should be destroyed. From the standpoint of economics, substantiated by observation and research, the broad-wing is an advantage to man. Because it frequents the unbroken forests during much of the year and has not made a reputation for itself as a killer of game or domestic fowl, it has not suffered the persecution of its relatives, the gaudier, more rapacious types, and will no doubt survive in numbers long after the others have become rare.

A few days later I went back through the woods to get a clear view of the nest from the rise behind it. One of the adults was sitting there calling quietly with the young clustered closely around. Something was wrong, of that I was sure, and then I saw the cause of their disturbance. A kingbird was perched on a branch about ten feet away. Suddenly it dashed toward the nest and with a swift dive struck the hawk between its shoulders, swooped clear, pounced again and again, and flew screaming jauntily back to its perch.

The broad-wing shrugged off each attack with nonchalance, sat on the edge of its nest, shoulders hunched, wings half spread, moving its head slightly from side to side. For hours, perhaps, it had been badgered by its assailant. Unable to fight because of the speed and swiftness of the kingbird, the hawk simply sat there protecting its young by using its body as a shield, but it was calm and unperturbed, talking softly to its frightened brood and assuring them that in time the irritation would pass.

Though here was guerrilla warfare, the constant harassing attack, the swift withdrawal only to attack again, tactics calculated to wear down the resistance and morale of a stronger, more powerful foe, the hawk never lost its poise, just sat there quietly waiting for the time when the tiny over-confident marauder must leave and feed its young in its own nest beside the beach.

After the kingbird had gone, the hawk took to the air, circled slowly and began to climb and soon was high overhead, soaring and wheeling and watching the earth below, the sparkling blue of the lake and its islands far to the northeast, the timbered ridges hemming it in, and directly below a smooth rocky point with a beach at its base and clump of dark timber between it and the aspen of the uplands.

A week later I found one of the young hawks on the ground, its head and throat partly eaten away. No doubt the bird had been trying out its wings when caught by a gust of wind, or in the confusion of a kingbird attack had lost its balance and tumbled to the ground, where it was easy prey for any passing forager. By late August the nest was empty, and, though I watched for the family many times, it was not until September that I saw them, and even then I was not sure.

I was on the end of the point watching the clouds through my glasses when suddenly I saw a group of four hawks soaring high overhead. Higher and higher they climbed, crossing each other's trails, until they were almost out of sight. Then, when only tiny specks against the blue, they reappeared in great circles, drifting, as one observer said, "Like dry leaves lifted and tossed and whirled on a zephyr of brisk autumn wind."

Many have marveled at the beauty of their soaring, but

none has given a more vivid picture than Lewis O. Shelley as he watched a family group of broad-wings over thirty years ago.

> *Slowly at first but gradually gaining momentum, the six birds on set pinions soared in and out among each other, round and round in a radius not greater than a quarter mile, lifting and ducking, volplaning and diving steeply toward the earth at varying angles, constantly rising nevertheless into the clear blue sky. As height was gained and maintained the dives and sails became swifter in the form of arcs and a series of dips and rises, a lower bird rising above them all, only to side-skip, arc, dive, and rise again and another repeating the maneuver, then another and another. As leaves on the wind current, there seemed no advantageous goal to their actions except to rise slowly at first and then with the gain of altitude swiftly up and up and finally lost to sight. Then in a few minutes they reappeared as tiny dots as they shot down plummet-wise, banked and regained altitude but steadily lowering in spectacular sweeps through the air and finally on set wings a sail that would take them to the summit of Smith's Hill and the dark wilderness fastness of Fuller Woods beyond.*

All the time I watched my four, I remembered Shelley's description and thought of the contrasting quiet existence of all broad-wings until the time of spring or fall. Then, shedding their modesty and coming into their own, they shared with the greater breeds the glory of their soaring, demonstrating for all the world to see that they too belong to blue skies and distances far above the earth, that they could sweep through the heavens with a grace and power and speed the others might well envy. What I saw that day and what I have seen many times since belied the slow, almost clumsy flight of summertime hunting, the sitting in wait on the ground instead of the swift torpedo attack, the commonplace appearance, the lack of bravado and color. Within those little hawks was hidden speed and audacity, beauty and grace, and, above all, sheer poetry of motion.

My four birds were still soaring the air currents, and I watched until they disappeared behind a bank of billowing cumulus. Already on their way, they would soon rendezvous with other family groups and then approach the gateways through the ridges in a swirling mass of thousands of wings, riding the glory of the skyways toward the south.

CHAPTER 13

LOGGING ROADS

I FOLLOWED an old logging road leading to the lake, one of the thousands of tote roads that wind here and there through the cut-over country in the north. In many places the almost forgotten trail was obliterated by alder brush and hazel and even good-sized trees, but for most of the way it was plain. Seen from the air.

these old roadways lie like a soft gray spider web over the land.

To the skiers they mean cross-country trails running wherever they wish to go, winding trails that lead up and down hills, through swamps and valleys, invariably following the finest routes for travel with grades, though meant for horses and sleighs, superb for slalom. I sometimes think as I come speeding down these roads from the ridges to the valley floors that the lumberjack swampers who laid them out must have had skiers in mind. How else could they have gauged to such a nicety the room and speed for a Christiania or a Telemark?

To the hunter they are important too, for the partridge come to them for gravel, succulent clover and grasses. The deer have learned that feeding is good along them too and that they are convenient trails to water.

To the trout fishermen, who are always searching for the spring-fed headwaters of streams, they are a godsend. What devotee of the elusive speckled trout but remembers long hikes through the dewy brush of old tote roads, and who hasn't caught a good one beneath the fallen timbers of some long-unused bridge?

I then followed an old roadway leading back of the cabin toward the high ridges overlooking the lake. From the topmost ledge I could see the islands and the sparkling blue of the water far into the north. While I rested there I imagined the big timber before the logging trails went in, just as it stands today along the Boulder River and the south shore of

Lac la Croix and on a few islands and forgotten pockets along the border, the massed ranks of tall pines close to the water's edge, the skylines through which the sun shines only at noon, the portages between the great boles and the forest floor clean of brush. But mostly I thought of the stillness there and the sense of smallness of a man and his canoe threading his way through the lakes and rivers hemmed in by the dark trees. I saw a vision of the brawling Kawishiwi and the Stoney and of all the north when the great unbroken stands were everywhere, two hundred miles of them from Rainy Lake to the shores of Lake Superior, a vast reserve that men could never harvest in a thousand years.

All that just seventy-five years ago, and now before me were birch and aspen, thickets of spruce and balsam woven together by the tough resilient hazel brush. Through the interlacing branches I could see the burnt-orange streamers of sunset and the blues and apple greens beyond. With a wall of pine and a solid horizon, I would have seen only a glow through the trees. Now there was light and color and space, but it would not be for long. Young pines were already shouldering their way above the rest. The old vistas were gone, but this was beautiful too, and with the legacy of logging roads the land was possibly more livable than before.

Years ago I visited a new logging area where lumberjacks were taking out timber by the old method of horse and sleigh. It was a thirty-below morning, and the steel runners screeched as they were drawn over the iced roads down to the river.

I stood to one side as a sleigh came by, saw the horses with steam rising above them and the skinner sitting astride his swaying load as nonchalantly as though there were no danger whatever. I heard his wild calls as he careened around a bend, wondered what would happen should a chain snap and that tremendous pile of logs break loose, saw his arrival at the flat below and the swift unloading on the landing at the riverbank. That kind of logging went on all through the northern states half a century or more ago and along the shores of Burntside Lake as well.

It was then they logged the point. The old stumps are still in evidence, some already crumbling and covered with moss, others sound and hard. Following the logging, fire came through, scarred the small pines that were left, and paved the way for the aspen and birch, the spruce and balsam that stood back from the shore. During those days the outlet of the lake was dammed and a sluiceway built to bring the logs over the rapids into a pool below. With the surge of the spring breakup, the flood waters that were held in leash coursed through the river and carried the logs to Shagawa and on to Winton and the waiting mills.

Because of the old dam, the level is somewhat higher now than before the logging, and along the bay several stumps stand in the water. At that time the beach was a landing-place for logs, and even now some are lying on the bottom as sound as the day they sank. The swimming-dock is built of them. I like to think they lay there, long and smooth and straight, waiting for me to find them and put them to use at last. One day while swimming we found a piece of rusty iron in the sand, part of an old hauling sleigh that knew the tote roads well.

Those were the days of high-water pants and calked boots and the jacks who came from the east following the lumber woods from Maine to the lake states and beyond. Wages were thirty dollars a month and found, and men lived in log bunkhouses, ate beans and sowbelly, and in the spring blew their wages in a week. Winton was headquarters in those days, and in the spring hundreds of jacks from the Stoney and the Kawishiwi and the Burntside country gathered at the mill town sprawled along the shore of Fall Lake. Those were roaring days, and in the little town were more saloons than eating-places and the hoosegow was always full. Even thirty years ago one could see the calk marks in the board sidewalks of the one main street, and the stories old-timers tell can curdle a modern's blood.

We regret the passing of those days, say that if the loggers had only known the value of scenery they might at least have saved the shorelines and blown up the dams after the logs were out. But we forget that then men thought of the wilderness as something to be eliminated and that forests existed only to be cut. No one had ever heard of recreational values or the conservation of natural resources. The pine stands were thought inexhaustible, and no one could have imagined a day might come when trees had other values than lumber. It was inevitable that most of the great forests should disappear and that today there are only a few places where they can still be found.

But the pioneer attitude survives and there are some today who still look at a tree as having just so many board feet and no other values. I visited with a cruiser of the old school not long ago while he was estimating the timber in a small stand on a neighboring lake. We stood in the shade of a big pine, one of the old ones, twisted and marked by lightning, with hardly a sixteen-foot log in its entire length. Punk knots indicating rot showed near the top, and there were scars of an ancient fire near its base. But the foliage was heavy and the wind murmured through it and I could hear the kinglets there.

"Take this one," said the cruiser as though reading my thoughts, "this is an old one and overripe, should be cut to make room for the young stuff coming underneath. Even the seeds aren't as good as they should be, and with the decay inside it's a nest for fungus and beetles. That tree is dangerous, ought to come out, and that's true of most of the big stuff left. People don't get any more pleasure from such a relic than they do from a healthy young tree." To emphasize his point, he took his ax and with two clean strokes cut out a chip of bark to mark it for the loggers coming in.

I tried to explain that, though I knew the needs of industry, such an old tree had its place and was worth more as a landmark than as timber; that knowing it was one of the last was justification enough for saving it; that, even though the rot was eating out its heart and it was marked by fire and disease, it had a value greater than anyone could estimate. But my arguments meant nothing to the viewpoint of my friend. He thought I was being sentimental about practical and obvious things and knew nothing of modern logging practice.

He might have lived a hundred years ago, would have seen eye to eye with the lumber barons who gutted the north and with the logger who a few years ago cut the big pine off one of the last untouched islands in Burntside Lake.

I skied over to that island one stormy night just before the logging outfit moved in; Oliver Island it was called, once the proud possession of a mining company and a landmark to all who knew the lake. It was dusk when I got there, and as I stood among the tall trees the snow drifted softly down. Those trees had been there for over two hundred years, were mature when the pines were crashing on other islands and on the mainland sixty years before. No fire had ever touched them because they were so far from shore that sparks and flames and burning bits of bark could never reach them. Here was a precious remnant of the Burntside that had been, a last museum piece that could never be replaced.

As I stood there, I could hear the soft moaning of the wind in the high dark tops and feel the permanence and agelessness of the primeval. In among those tall swaying trees was more than beauty, more than great boles reaching toward the sky. Silence was there and a sense of finality and benediction that comes only when nature has completed a cycle and reached

the crowning achievement of a climax, when all of the inter-
relationships of the centuries have come at last to a final
glory.

I paddled by the island in the spring and, while some of the
shoreline trees had been left, the old skyline was gone. Its
smoothly rounded dome with its wind-swept flags pointing
to the northeast was now a ragged fringe. In a bay were a
sawdust pile and an enormous mound of yellow slabs. The
interior ridges were bare and ugly and strewn with broken
branches and debris. Soon birches and aspen would fill the
gap, and in fifty or seventy-five years no one would ever
know that the island had once been different.

But for me it was a personal loss; I would remember how
it was that night when the snow was drifting down and I
listened to the great pines for the last time. The beauty and
the mystery of that moment was burned into my memory.
Could I have looked at the island from the standpoint of a
hundred years my sadness might have been lessened, but life
is all too short for that and I am not so wise. Though I knew
that time heals scars and islands raped will be green again,
that logging roads through fire and destruction would someday be charming runways through the woods and new vistas
be as beautiful as the old, still I could not wait. All I knew
was here and now.

The sun was down when I reached the point, and the
first stars were coming out. I stood on the bare rock at its
end and looked out across the channel toward the black mass
of the islands. For a day I had lived with a violent past, but

LISTENING POINT

Listening Point was the same as it had always been. Some things had changed there, it was true, but not the sense of mystery it gave me, nor the feeling of space and the unknown. It was still part of the old wilderness, and its sense of peace was still upon me.

CHAPTER 14

CANADA JACK

I<small>T WAS</small> high noon of a day in March and I sat with my back against a big pine and basked in the sun. Here on the south slope below the cabin the earth was already brown and dry, but on the north the drifts lay deep and there was still the feel of ice in the wind. A red squirrel scurried through the leaves hunting the cones it had buried the fall before and finally sat above me, enjoying the new warmth and aware of my every move.

I thought as I watched it how much a part of the pine it was, part of the rocks and the caribou moss, the balsams and the spruce, the wiry hazel brush and the whole ecological community there on the point. It belonged to its environment, would have been out of place anywhere else. To be sure, it could survive under different conditions, but here it was at home.

The squirrel took my thoughts to people and places I had seen all over the country, to those who really belonged and were at home. Canada Jack was one of these. About him was an air of authenticity and genuineness, nothing artificial or transient, just a quiet fitting-in and acceptance by the country of what he was. I first came to know him when he was guiding canoe parties into the wilderness lake regions of the Quetico-Superior. You had only to see him once to know that here was no summertime woodsman. About him was an unmistakable sense of belonging to the bush. It was in the way he walked and held himself and the outfit he wore. He had come in during the early logging after the turn of the century, had spent his early years in the big timber and on drives down the rivers. One of the best white-water men of those days, he could run a log through any rapids, pick the key timber out of a jam and make his way to the shore alive. To be a river pig in those days was something to be proud of.

He still wore the traditional outfit, spiked boots and stagged pants cut high above them, a black hat with a smooth undented crown tilted just so over his right eye, broad suspenders and a woolen shirt. But it was not what he wore as much as the way he wore it, the pride and cocksureness, his catlike walk, the look in his eyes of adventure and distance and long living out of doors.

Whenever I saw him down at the waterfront, the years rolled away and Jack was just off a drive and hitting town with the boys. Part of the whole north country, the roaring drives of spring, the mills now gone, the rocks and timber and frozen wastes of winter, he belonged to a bygone reckless era. Canada Jack, Austrian George, and Gunder Graves were of the old tradition, as much a part of the country as the forests themselves.

The squirrel chattered and scolded and pounded its feet on the branch of the pine as though applauding my decision to count Canada Jack and the boys as part of the country. It must have felt as I did—that, after all, there are only two kinds of people, those who belong and those who do not. You can always tell those who do, not by what they say but by how they make you feel. It makes no difference where they come from. You can recognize them instantly by a sign or a look. I recognized this same quality in a cowpuncher I saw one day in the little western town of Buffalo, Wyoming.

He had just ridden off the range and wore a working cowboy's clothes—plain cotton shirt and vest, a nondescript Stetson, a pair of chaps shiny with use, a saddle that knew the sagebrush and mesquite. He clattered into town, rode down the middle of the street looking neither to right nor left, oblivious of the shiny new cars and the neon signs.

As I watched him, summer traffic, the well-dressed tourists, and all of modernization disappeared. In their places were the false and unpainted fronts of a typical western cowtown, the hitching-posts outside The Last Chance Saloon, the long string of ponies standing head down switching their tails, waiting patiently for the time when they could ride the range again.

That cowboy was part of the old west, belonged not to the Buffalo of today but to the Chisholm Trail, the days of wagon trains, Deadwood Dick, and Wichita, Tombstone, and Rawhide Gulch. It was good to look at him and to know that he and his pony were real. They were as indigenous to the west as prairie dogs and the smell of sage.

I never bothered to find out his name or the outfit he rode with. It was enough to remember how he looked when he came down the street. He probably did not own an acre of the country he belonged to, but that made little difference. He owned the land far more than some who had deeds and titles and ranches stocked with white-faced steers. His was a kind of ownership that had nothing to do with abstracts, the kind that Canada Jack would understand.

There are many places where people have lived long enough to have sunk their roots deeply, who somehow have absorbed the character of the country they have chosen. I know parts of New England where the people are as native as the partridge in their upland pastures, places in the south where people have the feel of whippoorwills and mocking-

birds and magnolias in their blood, and in the west where
mountain ranges and purple vistas are a part of their lives.
Wherever you go, you will find them, but most always away
from the arterials and big towns, in the back country, where
they are still living close to the land. Theirs is a certain
contentment with things as they are, a perspective that comes
only with living in one place a long time, and a loyalty to the
old ways that fights change and modernization.

I know an old riverman down in the bottomland of the
Potomac. We sat outside his little cabin one evening and
talked of the days when he drove a mule team along the
towpath of the Chesapeake and Ohio Canal, and as we talked
the sound of traffic from the highway above was gone and
once again we were in the old south, the south of yellow
moons and coon-hunting and catfishing in the river, the
south of leisure where the war is still so close that Antietam
and Harper's Ferry seem like yesterday. There was no talk of
airplanes, the atomic bomb, or world affairs. Life was quiet
and good, and there had been little change.

"People wonder," he said, "why I don't want a highway
coming down the river bottom. Well, I'll tell you. We've
lived here a long time, and we like it. We like to sit in the
evening the way we're doing right now and listen to the
river. We like to see the moon coming up back of those hills
and remember that same moon was shining when General
Braddock built his road down below during the French and
Indian wars. I like to get out in my old flatboat and catch a
bass or a catfish when we need one, and in the fall those

mallards coming through the gap are something to hear. Those things I've known all my life, and what would we do, living in town? We belong here on the river."

He did not have to tell me more. Like Canada Jack and the cowpuncher out in Wyoming, he had stayed and learned to love the land and all it meant. He owned it, and the country owned him. He was as indigenous as the opossoms and persimmons along the river.

I wondered sitting there in the sun whether I could qualify with the rest. If the way I felt each time I approached my home country was any indication, then there was a chance. Not long ago, after a trip south, I had flown to an airport a hundred miles away, and all during the trip back to Ely and the point I was thrilled and excited. Every rock and tree, every muskeg and hill seemed friendly. It seemed to me that even the people I saw had a different light in their eyes. Memories of airplane terminals, big cities, and milling crowds faded swiftly, and in their place was the good warm feeling that here was where I belonged.

One memory that did not leave me was something I had seen in Tulsa a week before, a painting of an old Indian plowing a dry hillside in the southwest. He had just turned up a whitened buffalo skull and stood there in the sun looking at it and leaning on the handles of his plow. His horse, snowy white as he, stood head down, disconsolate and weary with the heat.

Then in the nebulous horizon of the painting I saw a vision—billowing cumulus clouds, stampeding buffalo, phantom horsemen in among them shooting their arrows as the dust rose high and the herd thundered across the prairie. Suddenly I was thrilled and the dry hillside forgotten, for the Indian looking at the sun-dried skull was seeing his youth in the buffalo country and remembering the wild freedom of his early days. In spite of the sadness of his end, this hunter of the plains had lived, and his was a satisfaction many never knew. Only he and those who had lived close to the land and had the feel of it in their blood could understand. To those who did not know, he was only local color, like Canada Jack, the cowpuncher, the riverman, but what they had was something many would give their all to find. Someday, perhaps, if I were patient and set my roots even more deeply in the north, I too might see the signs of recognition and know that I belonged.

My squirrel was getting restive, its hindquarters working up and down again. It had waited long enough, and it began to chatter and scold once more. At last unable to stand it any longer, it came down the trunk in short erratic jumps, chattering excitedly all the way.

"You belong, my friend," I told it. "Why should you be so perturbed when you know the point belongs to you? Here you are at home. While you may not have thought it out, you have a feeling for the land and the land for you. You don't have to travel to find what you need. You have it all right under your stamping feet. You are a native like the old Indian and Canada Jack and the cowpuncher and the riverman. You are a constant factor and a sort of leavening for transient America and, in a sense, a hope for its future. Time and place mean nothing to you, for you are already here and there is no other place you need to go.

"You may not know it, but you have a love for the land too, just like the rest, not a sentimental affection but a deep underlying need that puts you in a class by yourself. You have something more important than you will ever realize, something for which the rest of the world might well trade its wealth to own."

The squirrel looked me over disapprovingly, cocked one white-rimmed eye, and with a flurry of tail dashed across the leaves to a snowbank and then for the pines back of the cabin. The sun went under a cloud and suddenly there was a chill in the air. While it was out, it had blackened a spot in the ice of the bay and warmed the south slope, but now the leaves would swiftly turn crisp again, for there was still a month to wait for spring.

LISTENING POINT

CHAPTER 15

ROSE QUARTZ

THE rocky tip of the point is laced with intricate veinings of a lighter and different texture than the greenstone of the ledge. It is as though a thousand crevices had been cemented to hold together the cracked and broken surfaces before me. Some of the veins at their beginnings are several inches in width, fanning out eventually in delicate white traceries so minute they are all but lost in the darker matrix of the bedrock.

Those veins of quartz are evidence of an outpouring of hot solutions from the earth's molten interior. Streaming up from below, they had twisted and turned, explored every crevice and fissure, had flowed through and enmeshed the weathered surfaces of the greenstone, granite and schist that made up the end of Listening Point. In cooling their surge was slowed, and then miraculously crystals of quartz were formed, filling the fissures wherever the solutions had gone.

Near by are several jagged and rectangular bits of basic rock that once floated along in a tongue of lava as chips of wood might float in a creek. Breccias as they are called, they retained their shape because of rapid cooling at the surface.

Follow the shore to the north or south of the point, wherever you go is evidence of volcanic action and veining. Sometimes the quartz is milky white, sometimes like glass, but always beautiful, particularly when it is the color of old rose. Then to me it becomes a precious stone. Tinted by iron seepage from the hematite deposits that are found everywhere in this part of the north, rose quartz is found in most formations.

Quartz is always fascinating and, because it is one of the most common minerals on earth, one can find it on all continents. I have known the gray cherts and flints of England and Europe, the snow-white dikes and sills of the Canadian Shield from Lake Superior into the far northwest. For a hundred thousand years it was part of the culture of Stone

Age man, providing weapons, tools and ornaments. We use it today in greater and more infinite ways, for it is always beautiful and its crystals are very hard. Its affinity for color is endless; when violet it is called amethyst, when clouded or banded with various hues, agate, when red or brown it is jasper, and in shades of white or gray it is known as chert or flint. It is close to the morning hues of chalcedony and to the delicate opals with their reds and yellows, their greens and blues and moonlit lights. Even twin crystals have been found. When we think of its remarkable ability to absorb not only the colors of other minerals but seemingly all of the lights and variations of the spectrum, it becomes endowed with magic.

The most perfect crystal I ever saw was several inches in length, its hexagonal shape flawless and correct from the base to its sharply pyramidal top. Never had I seen one like this, never without some slight imperfection. I gazed at it in wonderment, for seldom are the large ones unblemished. This crystal came from the bottom of the famous Soudan mine some fifteen miles to the west of the point and two thousand feet underground.

The miner who was with me that day must have noticed my surprise.

"Nice one, ain't it?" he said. "Found it this morning in a pocket of ore, and when my light hit the cluster of crystals I never saw such a sparkle. There were lots of others," he said, "but I picked this one for the boss."

I took the crystal from him, turned it over slowly in my

hand, watching the play of light on its clear-cut rosy surface. Two thousand feet below ground level, and there it had lain since some ancient flow of possibly a billion years ago had forced its way through the beds of iron ore and then had cooled so slowly and under such constant pressure that the great crystal of quartz had been born, a crystal without disfigurement, one of those perfect creations man is always searching for but seldom finds. There it had been hidden long before his creation, had lain there unseen in all its beauty until my friend had caught it with his light and picked it up for his boss.

In the crevice before me the crystals were small, the result of an almost instantaneous change from hot to cold. The solutions responsible must have come to the surface to crystallize so minutely. I walked along the shore to a little promontory with a much wider veining running directly across it, a vein of rose, the identical shade of the great crystal of the Soudan.

As I sat there the whole violent story of the north came alive to me, for the quartz had been a part of it, in some form or other, during the three billion years or more since the whirling gaseous mass of the new planet began its condensation and the molten lavas that poured from its fiery interior flowed into the first primordial seas to make the Ely greenstone which underlies the point. Directly beneath me, below the granites of the Canadian Shield and the Soudan mine itself, lies the oldest rock in the world. This ancient basalt was solidified and compressed, flowed infinitely into layers, kneaded and ironed between other flows and against the basic masses which held it in, its characters so altered by heat, pressure and hot solutions that for a time its origin seemed a mystery. Its identifying color came as a result of complex chemical reactions that changed dark minerals to the light grayish green of chlorite.

The ancient Ely greenstone is the formation that cradled in gigantic folds the beds of iron that settled into the ooze of prehistoric seas. It held them close for a billion years while they were enriched by leaching, compacted by enormous pressures, folded again and again during volcanic periods when the tortured earth all but turned inside out. It was in such a cradle of greenstone that the great rose crystal was formed from one of the hot solutions that penetrated its iron beds. There at great depth and under incalculable pressures and a cooling that may have lasted centuries, the crystal grew and in growing took onto itself the color of the mineral around it.

There the crystal lay while the Laurentian Mountains reared their peaks and during the millions of years when the snow-capped ranges reached toward the sky. It was there while the mountains were being worn almost to the level of the seas by rains and snows and wind and by the heat and cold of forgotten eras. It was there while the eleven thousand feet of the Knife Lake formation were being laid down, the slates from the muds, the quartzites from the decomposed granites, the conglomerates from the pebbles and boulders of rivers and lakes. It lay there in the protecting embrace of the greenstone while all of this took place and while great tongues of molten lava coursing toward the surface miraculously passed it by, and the once proud Laurentians were worn to their base to become what is now known as the Canadian Shield.

But the greenstone lying massively beneath felt the weight of the deposition and there was a stirring and a shifting as the new formations pressed against it. Then came another uplift and the sedimentaries that came from the breakdown of the old mountains were folded and crumpled and again subjected to heat and pressure as once more batholiths of granite and gabbro pushed toward the surface and through the granites of former volcanic periods. Again came the weathering of the now complex and interwoven structures of the crust. Once-high horizons now filled the valleys and canyons, and then an arm of the sea moved in and all the land was covered except the Shield itself. It lay there like a rampart of the past, and the surf of the sea dashed itself against it.

In this sea some iron was deposited, the Biwabik formations of the Mesabi. Then again came violent outpourings of lava, some three hundred all told and over five miles in thickness. But so difficult had it now become for the new lava flows and solutions to force their way en masse to the surface that they worked themselves into fissures and cracks and faults, some finally oozing through to the now exposed surfaces before me. The vein of rose quartz on the point might well have been derived from one of these, but the flow that produced the crystal of the Soudan so far below the surface was even more ancient. The new eruptions were eroded once more, and with the attendant sinking of the earth's crust the sea crept in again clear to the shorelines of the old Shield.

For over half the geological history of the continent, the point has been near the center of volcanic action, racked by earthquakes, volcanic outpourings without number, mountainous uplifts, their inevitable erosion and the final invasion of the seas. The ancient granites and lava flows bore testimony to the violence of its past, but now for millions of years the area had lain undisturbed except by the forces of weathering, decomposition, and the grinding of glacial ice.

I sat on the end of the point and could see the striations of the last glacier, a mere ten thousand years ago, and knew that without its smoothing action the veining of quartz in the rock might not have been seen. It was as though someone had taken a rough section and run it through a polishing machine to bring out its color and structure.

Now was a period of erosion, but no one could tell what the future might hold in store. History would no doubt repeat itself and mountains rise again above the Laurentian peneplain. Once more might be far purple vistas, roaring canyons and alpine meadows above timber line. The ranges would yield as they always did to the assault of the elements, and inland seas might again encroach upon them.

Three billion years was too long a time to contemplate with wisdom and perspective. All I could do was be aware of the beauty around me. I could look at the rose quartz in its vein and delight in its color and the perfection of its crystals. I could explore the surrounding hills and find it in all its infinite variations as I did not long ago at the site of an abandoned mine shaft of the Vermillion gold rush of almost a century ago. I found it with the bluish-green stains of copper and the black of silver, even tiny yellow flecks of pure gold against the white.

These obvious beauties were important to me, and in searching for and finding them I knew joy and satisfaction, even though they played no vital part in the long story of the centuries. I thought of the rose crystal of the Soudan, a crystal that until the moment of its discovery was unknown to man. Who was wise enough to say it was unimportant? The miner who picked it up knew instinctively that here was something more than color or symmetry or a souvenir for his boss. Back of his reaction was a deeper intuitive perception than he realized, evidence of the endless search of all men for perfection and beauty, a goal possibly more significant than the fabulous beds of iron that had hidden the crystal so long.

Today is one of glorious October, and Listening Point is strewn with red and yellow leaves. The veins of quartz are partly covered with them, and where they are rose, the color blends with the warm tints of autumn. This I can enjoy without perspective, but, knowing the past, the great forces that made them possible and the eons that shaped them, I can look with even greater wonderment at all that is about me.

CHAPTER 16

BEAVER CUTTING

J̲UST off the point a small aspen had been felled. Though there were no beaver dams near by, none of their houses in the bay or toward the river, the tooth marks were fresh and plain. This must have been a lone beaver cruising along the shore with an eye for a succulent bit of food, an old bachelor perhaps, shunned by his tribe and living by himself. The top had been carried into the water, and only part of the trunk had been gnawed.

This was the sign of Castor canadensis that men had followed for three hundred years as they followed the lure of gold. When they carried the emblem of France, the fleur-de-lis, into the hinterlands, it was the beaver that led them on. Pelts were so highly prized during those days that they were legal tender and men counted their wealth by how many they owned. Blankets, guns and supplies were rated by their worth in fur, and even today the famous Hudson's Bay blankets carry the traditional mark of three or four points, indicating the number of hides it took to buy them. While there were other furs, the beaver set the standard and it was in search of them that expeditions set out for the northwest.

Radisson and Groseilliers are thought to have visited the country north of Lake Superior as far back as 1660 searching for new trapping-grounds and Indians who would trade. From that time until well after the Revolutionary War this was prized beaver country, and no one knows what fortunes in fur were packed across its portages to the waiting flotillas of canoes on Lake Superior. It was the beaver that opened up the routes of exploration.

By the last quarter of the nineteenth century, however, the trade had declined and beavers all but disappeared in the Quetico-Superior country. It may have been due to over-trapping, lack of food, or possibly disease. Not until the aftermath of logging and its inevitable fires that brought back their favorite food, the aspen and birch, did they return. By the 1920's they were well on the way, but not until 1939 was there an open season on the United States side of the border. Between that time and 1955, according to Milton H. Stenlund, area biologist, 166,785 beavers were taken in Minnesota with a total value of three million dollars. It is of interest to note that the last year of record, 1955, showed the most pelts, a total of 22,500, proof of the durability of the species.

Beavers are highly important to the ecology of the north. Their ponds provide habitat for black mallards and wood ducks, forage and refuge from flies for deer and moose. Flowages and dams act as flood controls and water storage, and foresters depend on them during fires as barriers against the flames.

Trout fishermen are divided in their opinions. Some say that streams are improved because back of every dam is a pool. Others bemoan the fact that dams eliminate fast water, all the ripples and natural swirls that harbor trout, and that eventually all trees beside a stream are either cut by beavers or killed by their flooding.

The fact that an adult beaver might down as many as a hundred trees in a year shows what damage to forest cover can take place, explains why colonies are doomed almost as soon as they are established because of the vast quantities of food they need. After a few years all trees within reach are gone, including stands at the far ends of canals leading from the ponds. Then the colony must move to an untouched area, to return only when new growth has come back around the homes they have abandoned.

While they have enemies—wolves, coyotes, and bobcats, and in the old days the wolverine—because of the nature of their habitat they have little to fear. Nothing can touch them all winter long while their houses are frozen solid, nor during the summer if they stay close enough to water. Their greatest enemies are disease and lack of food. When fires are kept under control and the pine and spruce grow tall, the beavers face their end. Only when aspen and birch come in do they thrive for long, and so it must have been in the early days. Tremendous fires between the stands of virgin pine produced their breeding-grounds, and when these were exhausted the trade declined.

I examined the fresh cutting, the little pile of white chips that lay around the base of the stump, the peeled branch that lay silvery white in the water just offshore. Across the channel to the west was a colony I knew, one of hundreds that now dot the canoe country. It was high time I visited the beavers again, and now I had a visit to return. I paddled across the bay and, at the mouth of a creek coming down from the northwest, beached the canoe and hiked upstream until I came to the dam. It was late when I got there, and the water lay like a pool of wine among the birches. The house rose in conical splendor in the very center of the pond, the dam curving smoothly against the flow. Though it was not large, generations of beavers had worked there building this wilderness bridge across the creek. From its mud-encrusted walls came a constant trickling, the overflow from the pond above. The water was high and into the trees, and dead birches stood knee deep around the edges. They stood there white and broken and ghostlike against the wall of black spruces behind them.

I thought as I sat there of the tremendous dam on Longstaff Creek to the south. It is very old, and no beavers have been there for many years. A quarter of a mile in length, it is wide enough on top for a team of horses and a sleigh, and the grassy meadow above is over a mile across. That dam was of the past, dated from the days of Radisson and Groseilliers. The meadow with its black rich soil might someday make a farm, but now it lies unused with the little creek winding lazily through it on its way to the lake.

To make the beavers work on the dam below me, I broke through its crest, tore out several poplar sticks and stones and kicked away the mud. Soon the water surged noisily through the gap, a challenge the beavers could not ignore.

I climbed the hillside then and settled down to wait. Perhaps they might cut some aspen right before me, drag the branches to the dam, and carry armfuls of mud to hold them down. Suddenly a head showed near the break and a beaver climbed out and made a survey. Soon there were others, and then I heard the sound of a tree being felled. I could not see, for it was dusk, but there was a swish, and a small tree fell to the ground; more gnawing and beavers were swimming toward the break with branches held firmly in their teeth.

Up into the gap they went, then, with great splashing and commotion, dove below for mud. After a while there was no further sound of rushing water, and I could hear the beavers swimming and working their way up the canals toward the aspen grove and coming back again to the storage pile beside the house.

As I sat there on the hillside watching the changing color in the pool, my notebook was forgotten and I was conscious only of the wild and placid beauty of the scene below. Such scenes had taken place before Columbus ever dreamed of a new continent. Here was primitive America, and in this little valley there had been no change. While the continent had been tamed and harnessed to the will of man, here time stood still.

Suddenly it was dark on the hillside, but I sat a long time listening to the activity below me, stayed until the dankness of the beaver pond and the lushness of the flooded shores seeped into my consciousness. Then back over the darkening trail I went, back to the canoe and to the point. By the light of the fire I opened my notebook, found only one notation: "Beaver Pond," and that was all—not one scientific observation. But I had paid my respects and lived for a while in the beaver country of my travels and thought of old Beaver Creek, which runs past my home and through the little town where I live.

That creek is marked by a fringe of alder and willow winding its way through the valley. From my home I can see the bog from whose seepage it stems. Now it is thickly grown with ash and spruce and tamarack, and along its edges are hosts of invading aspen and birch. But there are places in the deep shadows where remnants of the old cushion of sphagnum still hold on and where the earth trembles when one walks near by. But this is only in the spring after the melting of the snows. Only then does it resemble its former sodden virility.

The ash trees are large now, thirty feet or more in height, and they stand as ash should with their roots in the cold acidity they love. But the creek that once foamed out is changed, and only for a few days in May is there any flow at all. I followed Beaver Creek one day last spring and found that it disappears where it enters the town, and the old stream bed where it once rollicked merrily as it raced down the ridges to Shagawa Lake is gone. Not a trace of the water or its course remains.

When men first came to the Vermillion Range to dig for iron, the creek emerged clear and cold from the swamp, skirted a ridge of towering red pines, and lost itself in a beaver pond backed up against the hill. Here it dropped its silt, trickled through the dam, and passed the mining camp. For untold centuries humus and peat had accumulated there as it had in the old meadow of Longstaff Creek to the west. Now it enriches a hundred garden plots and lawns where the pond once stood.

Some years ago I stopped on a street where workmen were excavating for the foundation of a house. They were down three feet or more and were having trouble with their digging, for their shovels had uncovered an old beaver dam whose sticks buried in the muck were as solid as the day they were laid down.

That was one of the dams that held the waters of the pond during the days of the mining camp, the dam that marked the outlet of the creek when the pine stood dark and brooding on the ridge to the south. Then caribou and moose came from the hills to drink and feed there and ducks nested in the sedge along its borders. That was seventy years ago. Now on the site of the old beaver pond are streets and pretty ranch-type houses and shade trees planted in neat rows. What is left of the creek runs into a drain at the lower end of the avenue, and small boys play there in the spring.

Not long ago I walked down to the creek bed just below the swamp, stepped across on a couple of whitened stones where once was a swirling rapids. It was midsummer and there were horse tracks through the mud; algae and green scum filled them, and mosquito larvae wriggled to the surface in each little puddle. The water lay dead and stagnant in the heat.

And while I stood there I pictured the old Beaver Creek pouring smoothly from the cold springs and seepage of the swamp, flowing past the pine ridge, spreading out and losing itself in the pond, and at last, as though glad of release, trickling through the dam and laughing its way through the camp and down to the lake.

Sometimes in the spring when snows are melting fast and the gutters of the new streets are running full, nights when there is the music of running water everywhere, I feel as though the old creek had come to life again and was singing its way through the clearing of the first settlement. I think of the men who knew it then and of their dreams of the fortunes they hoped to make and the city they would build there. Now they are gone; the creek is gone, and only a few remember.

But the beavers are still in the country. They do not regret the passing of Beaver Creek, for they own many others all over the area. The lone bachelor who cut the aspen off the point may have been exploring for the site of a new colony. Perhaps he would decide to pick the bay, with its fringe of young aspen along the shore. I could spare some there, and all I would ask in return would be a chance to watch them in the summer evenings playing around the house and to hear the pistol crack of slapping taiis upon the water. After all, the bay belongs to them far more than to me. I had just come, but they have been there thousands of years.

Over toward the far point where the lone pine stood, I heard a faint splash and saw a spout of silver as a beaver slapped its tail and dove, and then I followed the wake of its swimming far toward the open, watched until it merged with the sunlit ripples and was gone.

CHAPTER 17

KING'S POINT

THE scraggly little pine on
the end of the point belongs to the memory of Walt Hurn.
It is bent and twisted, had once been flattened against the
rock by some storm on the past, only to point upward again.
Now it is anchored in a cleft of the greenstone, having only
a few tortured branches that have survived the winds. They

138

are gnarled and out of shape, but hold their tufts of needles defiantly against the sky. The little pine is part of Listening Point and of my memories as well. It belongs there, would be out of place in a fertile protected valley. Conditioned by the past, it can never grow tall and straight like the rest, but will always reveal its background.

Walt Hurn, once Canadian ranger at King's Point just to the north, was like that pine, for he too had weathered the storms and in the process had become just as gnarled, indestructible and indigenous. Although it has been thirty years since I checked in with him on my way to Quetico Provincial Park as a young guide, I can still see the great spare shoulders bent desperately over a report, the rootlike fingers moving slowly across the page with a tiny stub of a pencil all but lost between them, fingers used to rocks and boulders, to ax work and the heavy packs of portages. During those days he was King's Point, part of the log ranger station nestled under the tall Norways, part of the brooding cliffs of Ranger's Bay behind and the broad sweep of water toward Jackfish and the outlet. The fluttering Union Jack was more than a symbol of authority and an outpost of the Empire. To me it meant Walt Hurn. Like the gale-beaten pine beside me, he belonged to the Canadian bush, or so I thought, a ranger of the old school who had taken over his post long before anyone ever thought of tourists or wilderness canoe trips and when blank spaces on the maps still meant the unexplored. When he used to talk about going outside, I never took him seriously. All woodsmen talked that way, but when the time came there was always some excuse for staying on.

"Someday," he'd say, "I'm going to turn in my ranger's badge and head for Merrie England, buy me a little garden spot near the coast, and raise the prettiest flowers on the island."

I used to laugh at him. "Walt," I would say, "you know you couldn't stand it over there. This is your country," and then we would walk around and look at all he had done there, and all that time I did not know how he felt.

To me the idea that he could transplant himself to some pocket-sized garden plot with clipped hedgerows after knowing the wilds and the freedom of the north seemed incongruous. I could have as easily imagined taking the twisted pine from its rocky holdfast and planting it in the rich soil of Kew Gardens outside London.

Because I was young and did not know that men are unlike trees, that within them is more than fiber and resin and the will to live, I thought it would be that way with Walt. I did not understand that what had made his lonely station different from any other in Quetico Park and possibly in the whole of Canada was a core of loyalty to another way of life that the wilds could never quite erase, that in everything he did his memories came to life. This was the real Walt Hurn and a man I did not know.

All of the crew of hard-bitten young guides felt the same about King's Point. There is something different about jumping-off places, no matter where they happen to be. Whenever one leaves security and says good-by to the familiar, events seem to be more sharply etched. People stand out as types, and everything is colored more vividly. But even though we were used to such places all over the map, Walt Hurn and his station were different from the rest. Now that I look back and realize what the old ranger did there, it all fits into a pattern, from the way he treated us to the many things he did that made King's Point what it was.

No matter if we had been gone for weeks or months and this was our first exciting touch with civilization, he never so much as lifted an eyebrow or let on that our arrivals were anything out of the ordinary. We were puzzled at times, for coming out of the bush is no light experience when you are young and full of the joy of life. Now I know it was part of the whole picture he had created there, part of a background of quiet conservatism we knew nothing about. To him our adventures were all in the day's work.

To eyes that for long had seen nothing but the wild, his little spot of grassy turf between the beach and the cabin was exciting. It wasn't a clipped lawn or laid out in any particular way, just a bit of bluegrass that had taken root beneath the Norways, a tough bit of sod that somehow never needed cutting. We spent many hours there waiting for a tow, lying on our backs looking up through the tops of the pines, pure luxury after the rocks of portages and the torrent-washed bottoms of river beds.

One of the many things that impressed us at King's Point was its order and cleanness. Starting down at the beach with its white sand and gravel and its two trim canoe rests, this cleanness spread up over the point itself, took in the **wood-pile**, the toolshed, the cabin, clear back into the timber. Even under the trees not a cone seemed out of place.

But the log cabin was something to see. Just being clean would never do. The floor was always scrubbed snowy white, and no paint or varnish was ever allowed to touch it. Even though it would have saved much labor and preserved the wood, we had a feeling that Walt considered such artifice a sign of weakness and lack of character.

Because of his passion for order, there was about King's Point a perennial Sunday-morning freshness. Sometimes we thought he overdid it, that there was no excuse for having a floor so white we felt we must take off our boots before stepping inside, but all of this had a place there and an effect on every one of us. We never dreamed of arriving without having washed our torn wilderness outfits and shaved our beards. King's Point demanded nothing less.

You would never believe that a garden patch up there in the wilds meant very much, but it did—more, in fact, than most of us ever cared to admit. Even though we did not know its real meaning to Walt Hurn, the impact of it was inescapable, and after each trip we looked forward to seeing it.

Coming out of the bush where all vegetation runs riot to suddenly find clean gravel walks, vegetables in straight rows and a profusion of flowers, when for a long time we had known only muskeg, rocks, and timber, did something to us.

I used to walk between the beds back of the cabin, tramping almost reverently down the paths in my hobnailed boots, marveling at the sky blue of larkspur and delphinium, the burnt orange of poppies, and the crimson of hollyhocks and zinnias. Somehow up there those colors were a miracle; not that I was a flower-lover particularly, but order and color were such a change from what I had seen. Back home I would have taken it for granted, but on King's Point it was entirely different.

A little pansy bed lay right in front of the cabin. It had stakes driven all around it to keep out the rabbits, and all season long it was filled with bloom. I could never resist the rich velvet flowers that grew there; coming up from the beach I always picked one to wear in my buttonhole, and if I failed to make my choice, soon after my arrival Walt reminded me. He was pleased that I noticed his tiny bed.

The luxuriousness of his flowers and garden was due to the compost pile beside the cabin, and to him compost was more precious than anything on the point. No bit of garbage was ever wasted, no leaves or grass burned, no fish entrails, carcasses, or offal of any kind were buried elsewhere. Everything went into that soft black mound.

"Humus," he used to say, crumbling the stuff in his great hard palm, smelling it, gloating at its dark richness. "There's the stuff that makes 'em grow, there's where you get the color."

The compost heap was typical of Walt and in a way was the key to everything he did. His creation back in the wilds of the border country was a bit of the beauty of the old England he had left behind.

143

There were many other things that over the years worked themselves into our memories: the deep-dish blueberry pies he baked, the sourdough pancakes we had beside the crackling kitchen stove in the dark of a morning, stormy nights when we'd roll up on the floor and listen to the crash of thunder and the waves down at the beach. Then, too, the rocky islands coasting the bay in front, and the roar on quiet nights of Basswood Falls on the route to Lac la Croix.

Yes, there was much to remember, for King's Point was beautiful even as it is today, but it was not a matter of beauty alone or the fact that here was a garden in the wilderness and that it was clean and immaculate. The important thing, I realize now, was that Walt Hurn was there, and it never occurred to any of us that someday it would change.

That was why it was such a shock one fall to learn that he was coming down, that he had turned in his badge and was leaving the Service just as he had said he would and was going back to Merrie England. Somehow we could not believe it, for it seemed to our young minds an unnatural thing to do. The day he was scheduled to come down from King's Point was a blue-gold one in October. We were down at the dock on Fall Lake, had been there most of the morning talking about the tourist season just past, of guiding prospects for the coming year, and watching the head of the lake for the first telltale spout of spray.

"There she comes," someone said.

We looked up toward the narrows, saw a launch coming around the point, spewing the waves before it, slapping its way gaily into the morning blow. It bore down the channel and headed directly toward us. One passenger, a pack, and a couple of big boxes on the deck, and that was all.

Until the last moment we hoped that the launch would be empty, but now we knew we were wrong. There was no mistaking the broad-shouldered frame, the weathered old hat, or the way he stood. He waved once, got ready for the landing. The bow swung in with an extra flourish, gears ground in reverse, and the boat warped into position. Willing hands tied it fast.

After we had his outfit on the dock, Walt stood for a moment looking up the lake toward the Four Mile Portage across American Point.

"Well, boys," was all he said, "it's the last time. Now for Merrie England," and the old twinkle was in his eyes—just as matter-of-fact and casual as that, just the way he used to say good-by in the old days, no fuss or sentiment, merely a checking out as though he would be back in a couple of weeks.

A truck was waiting at the road. He climbed in, waved once, and suddenly was gone, and with him the King's Point we had known.

The twisted little pine rustled in a sudden breeze, and then the wind came strongly and the turf with its layer of brown needles and silvery caribou moss moved gently above the root and the crevice of the rock. It would always bring me memories of Walt Hurn and the days when I thought that he too belonged to the rugged land of the Quetico.

CHAPTER 18

THE WHISTLE

THERE was no sound, no lapping of the waves against the rocks, no rustling of leaves or moaning of wind through the trees, one of those times when all seems in suspension and even the birds are hushed. While I sat there on the end of the point, my senses all but fused with the enveloping silence, I gradually became conscious of a soft undercurrent of sound like the coming of a wind from far away or something long remembered. But as I looked around me there was no roughening of the water or even the slightest swaying of tree tops and the quiet was as intense as before.

In spite of the fact I saw no change, the undercurrent persisted. Then suddenly I knew, as the long-drawn wail of a steam locomotive drifted over the hills and valleys from the south. Until that moment I had forgotten that just a few miles away was a railroad and a paralleling highway as well. On other days, with a wind and the sounds of the forest to screen it from my hearing, it had not been perceptible.

As the train whistled again and again with the muffled roar of cars growing more and more distinct, I wondered for the first time since coming to the point if I had chosen well, if the railroad and the highway might not destroy the very essence of the sanctuary I had found. Another whistle farther away, plaintive and dying now, and the sound of the train was gone. There was only the cushioned humming of traffic from the road.

Once long ago on another point far to the north and after weeks of wilderness travel I had heard the same sound, but then it seemed entirely different. We were camped that night within a few miles of the steel, as we called the railroad back in the bush. Our maps told us where we were, but it was hard to realize we had come so close, for until then it had seemed almost unattainable. For a long time we had heard only the sounds of animals and birds, the wind in the trees, the thunder of rapids, and the crashing of waves. We had talked about coming out to the steel as though it were the most wonderful thing in the world, which in truth it was to a bush-weary crew. We knew we would reach it if we kept on packing down the portages and following the waterways, but the goal was always far away, and the longer we were gone the more unreal it actually became.

Then one night after supper came the whistle of a train, the same long-drawn musical notes I had just heard off the point, a sound so foreign to the life we had known and so filled with meaning that sleep was forgotten. Never before, it seemed, had we listened to a harmony that meant so many things—friends and loved ones, towns and cities and all they denoted. We sat there and none of us said a word, each man occupied with his own thoughts and dreams. How we strained to catch those last haunting notes, and how excited we were at the realization that at last we were going outside. The final note was like the call of a loon, the mournful wail of a lone bird with the darkness settling down, but this time there was no sadness in the sound. In it was a note of finality, for it wrote the finish to our cruise and all we had experienced together.

Until then we had gone about the ordinary routine of wilderness travel taking everything for granted, making the best of discomforts, spending our evenings and stormy days busying ourselves with the endless details necessary to keep an outfit in traveling order, but now all of this was unimportant. The shaping of the new paddle could wait, the rip in one of the tents, the broken tumpline, the ax that needed sharpening. Suddenly impatient at the seemingly senseless delay of nightfall, we were counting the hours until dawn. To a man, we would have packed up and traveled in the dark if our leader had said a word. All that counted now was getting in, though we knew that in a short time we would be ready to hit the trails again.

And now on another point of rock I had listened to the same music, remembering all the mixed-up feelings of my youth, emotions and hopes that in the light of years and a maturer perspective seemed quite different from what they were then. That night of long ago, after the fire had died and camp was asleep, I had lain awake thinking of many things. Quietly I had crawled out of my bag and tiptoed down to the overturned canoes near the shore. I remembered the moment clearly, how the Big Dipper hung and the sliver of a new moon over the spruces. I went around and looked at the old battle-scarred canoes, the one that was heavy on the portages, the one with the cracked ribs that we had almost lost in a rapids, one whose gunwale the porkies had chewed. Sometime during the coming day we would leave them and scatter to the four winds, and the life that meant so much to us, the companionship we had known, the banter, the fun and hardships, would be ended. It was sad to think of these things, for in the wilds you become welded not only to the outfit itself but in a strange way to those you live with. But, even so, this moment was the one we had worked for, this the reward for long days on the trail.

While I thought of that night of long ago, the dark had come to Listening Point and the Big Dipper hung exactly the way it had then. Nothing had really changed at all, for there was the lake with its star shine, there the massed outline of the far shore. The only difference was the fact that, instead of being happy and thrilled, I was now vaguely disturbed. I had chosen the point fully aware of its closeness to civilization. All I had actually wanted there was a window through which I might glimpse at times the wilderness I had known and recapture perhaps some of the feel of the country I had traveled almost to the Arctic. I had accepted my road, motor boats and near-by cabins, and the realization that many times the silence would be shattered. I knew that, while the point was relatively unchanged and like ten thousand such points far to the north, it still was not the wilderness, did not have the element of isolation that only great distances could provide. Then why, I asked myself, was I troubled at hearing the sound of a train?

The leaves of an aspen began to whisper in a sudden breeze and the soft humming from the south was gone. A loon called wildly from the open lake, and miraculously everything seemed as it was before. The point was still part of the wilds, but I could not forget the whistle and sat there in the dusk wondering if it could ever be quite the same.

A few months before I had met a party of Cree Indians along the far reaches of the Athabasca over a thousand miles to the northwest. They too were camped on a stark and lonely point, as much a part of the beauty and silence of their land as the caribou themselves. How would they have reacted to the whistle? Could they understand its real meaning as I did? Could they possibly comprehend Thoreau's famous dictum that "In wildness is the preservation of the world"? I wondered as I sat there, knowing full well if those Crees were taken from their land and transplanted to some city, something within them would die and, while they could not explain their dependence, the ancient need was there. Only through my own personal contact with civilization had I learned to value the advantages of solitude. Without that experience they could not realize how man in an industrial age might need the very background of the life that was theirs. Nor did I know this truth thirty years before when I first heard that train whistle after a long time in the bush.

While I sat there thinking of the Crees and my own early reactions I seemed to hear the whistle again, but now it had assumed a somewhat different note and in the sound I heard something that had not been there before: a deeper meaning than the train itself, one that encompassed man's inventive genius and all the realms of his exploring mind, a sound that was responsible for my own background and everything I knew and felt. And then the realization dawned on me that only because of its connotations and the contrasts that had been mine could I really appreciate the wilds and their importance to mankind.

A motor boat roared down the middle of the lake, its throttle wide open, headlight knifing through the dark. It headed into the west, slapping smartly over the waves, made a wide careening turn near the first islands, and came directly toward me. Fascinated, I watched as it sped by and disappeared. Its roar grew less and less and at last was swallowed by the north channel. Then came the wash, long rollers whispering and chuckling along the shore. Longer and longer became the intervals between them, and at last, like an inaudible sigh, the quiet returned. Again I was disturbed, and again I remembered. This too had the same meaning as the whistle itself.

But there would be many times in the months to come when the lake would be completely undisturbed. I remembered skiing with streamers of snow writhing and twisting and turning red and violet in the slanting rays of the setting sun, days when even the most ardent ice fisherman would not venture forth, the time I explored the river when the little cabin at its outlet was sealed and cold and timber wolves had run across the smooth hard drifts of the clearing.

I thought of the fierce storms of late October and November just before the freezeup, with the ducks heading south, snow drifting quietly down, and no one left in the whole country to take away the feeling of the wild; the time before the spring breakup with its black treacherous ice, and the insulation that all harsh weather gives the north. Knowing this, I was ashamed of my resentment at intrusions no matter what they might be. I should be able to listen to all of them with equanimity, attune my mind and thoughts so I would hear them as they should be heard.

Some other day when the wind was right or the quiet as

THE WHISTLE

breathless as this afternoon, I would hear the train again and the steady humming of traffic from the highway. I would remember the time I heard the whistle after that long expedition of years ago and the joy it had brought me then. No longer would I be disturbed, for I would listen now with understanding, knowing what it really meant. Without that long lonesome wail and the culture that had produced it, many things would not be mine—recordings of the world's finest music, books holding the philosophy, the dreams and hopes of all mankind, a car that took me swiftly to the point whenever I felt the need. All these things and countless others civilization had given me, and I must never again forget that because of the wonders it had wrought this richness now was mine.

The next time I heard the whistle I would think of all these things. The very presence of the railroad and highway over the ridges to the south gave new significance to wilderness, to solitude and the entire concept of Listening Point.

CHAPTER 19

THE PORTAGE

THE portage lay in the end of the bay, and there a battered white sign was nailed to a tree. As the canoe slipped beside a log we stepped into the shallows and lifted out the packs. The sign was broken in half, torn no doubt by a curious bear, weathered and beaten by the wind, but on it were the names of voyageurs who had gone before.

THE PORTAGE

I stood for a long time looking at that sign as I have looked at hundreds in the wilderness lake country here and far to the north, and marveling as I always do that somehow I had arrived at a known and definite point on the map. That morning the portage had seemed far away from the point. There had been miles of open water, narrows and islands to traverse, and now, at last, here it was exactly where it was supposed to be.

The trail was narrow, no more than a foot in width, for men, like animals, in the wilds make little paths. It was carpeted with pine needles and the leaves of aspen and birch, packed hard by the feet of generations of travelers. It led between rocks, around hummocks, skirting wet places, using logs for bridges where the muck was soft, over windfalls and around clumps of blocking trees. This primitive path was part of the great network that laces together the waterways, a connecting link between two lakes, but in its simplicity and the way it threaded through the woods it was typical of all the wilderness trails in the world.

The first man who found his way through here had followed perhaps the trails of moose or caribou, for they also travel from lake to lake, but because they seldom follow the shortest route he was forced to branch off and head for the closest point of the shore. No doubt he climbed a tree or a ridge to get his bearings, then returned and blazed his way or broke off branches to guide him back.

The next man through followed the marked trail with more ease, broke more branches, slashed a few more blazes

155

on the trees, might even have cut a windfall blocking the way. From then on each traveler improved the portage a little more until at last it was as definite and direct as the terrain would allow. After many years of use, someone with more ambition than the rest chopped out the great logs that men had scrambled over and finally tacked a sign on a tree near the water so that canoes coming in would see it from the lake.

This portage was primitive, as all such trails are, the result of steady improvement by all who came that way, and dedicated to a type of use that belonged to the wilderness. To straighten out the bends and loops that had become a part of it because of obstacles avoided, to remove all natural hazards and even to mark it too well would have taken something from it, just as an old and winding road changes in character when all the curves are eliminated in the interest of speed.

For countless thousands of years men have followed such trails. It is instinctive to pack across them, and you bend and weave, adjust your weight and balance, do all the things your subconscious experience tells you to do without realizing exactly what is happening. In the low places your feet feel for the rocks and tussocks of grass, for the sunken logs that keep you from bogging down. You approach them as a horse approaches a bridge, with the same awareness of danger. Over the rocks and beside a rapids where a slip might plunge you into a torrent or over a cliff, your feet are your eyes as they have always been where the going is rough.

Once I followed one of the traces along the crest of the

downs in the south of England. It was high above the villages and above the woods, wound its way along the tops of the open hills as it had for many thousands of years. This was one of the trails of the ancient tribes that inhabited the island long before the Romans came, long before any of the roads they built. The Celts traveled high, the better to watch their enemies. Up there along the crest they could see far and the going was clear. The men who followed those traces picked their routes of travel like wolves who follow open ridges in the north. Along them are the Druid circles and ancient places of worship and sacrifice, and, like portages, they too are narrow and winding and as natural as the game trails they might have been during England's past.

There are also the walking trails across the fields of England, the stiles over fences and hedgerows, trails that because of their historic value are recognized as legal highways that cannot be blocked by owners of the land. These traces and foot paths were the first roads. Dignified by tradition and centuries of use, they are part of the cultural background of the people.

On the North American continent these traces are also in evidence, not only the portages between lakes and along the river systems but trails through great areas of terrain. To these belong the Iroquois War Road from New England to the south, the Natchez Trace from Tennessee almost to the Gulf of Mexico, the Wilderness Road of Daniel Boone, the Oregon Trail, and the Santa Fe, all walking trails for warriors and pioneers.

In time many of them became roads and later the arterials of today. Cities were built along them, just as the villages of England strung themselves like beads along the ancient traces of the downs. Most of those old trails are gone now, but, for those who know where to look, remnants can still be found and from the soaring crests of the new highways one can catch the vision of the men who marked them first.

I have known portages all over the country, the short unimportant ones not rating a name, the difficult ones oftentimes of great historic interest. There is Grand Portage, once gateway to the northwest, the nine-mile carry around the brawling rapids of the Pigeon River where it empties into Lake Superior; Staircase Portage just above, where voyageurs built a rugged stairway down a steep cliff; Frog Skin Portage from the Churchill to the Sturgeon Weir, where the Crees as a mark of derision stretched a frog skin and hung it there to show those who had not learned to stretch a beaverhide, that this was how it was done. The legends about them are many, for it was here men met on the long routes they must follow in the north.

I thought of these things as I tossed the canoe onto my shoulders and started across the portage. Countless feet had trod it smooth long before I came. During the logging days part of it had been used as a tote road, but now it was grown to brush and trees again. It is a long carry and uphill most of the way and I thought I could make it without a stop, but near its crest I weakened, placed the bow of the canoe in the crotch of a birch, and rested. Then almost imperceptibly the trail led down the ridge, and it was then I caught the first sight of blue, just a glimmer through the trees but enough to take away the weariness and fill me with the same old joy I had known thousands of times in the past, an elation that never grows old and never will as long as men carry canoes and packs along the waterways. In spite of the labor, it is this that makes portaging worth while. There is no substitute. If someone transports your outfit for you, it is lost. It colors your entire attitude, makes each lake reached mean infinitely more. It is exactly like climbing a mountain. You could be dropped there by helicopter or view it from a low-flying plane, but unless you have climbed cliffs, scaled precipices, and inched your way upward, fighting for breath, you have no understanding of the satisfaction of the first long look into space. So it is with portages and the first sight of glorious blue through the trees. When I dropped my canoe at last into the water and stood there puffing and blowing and looking down the expanse of the lake, my feeling of accomplishment was one that had been earned.

But just walking across a portage has its compensations too. In a canoe, even though you slip quietly along the shores, you still cannot achieve the feeling of intimacy that is yours on the ground. There you hear sounds that are lost on the water, see things that until then have been hidden. After hours of paddling, a portage brings new muscles into use, and how delightful to rest with your back against the canoe, doing the aimless things one does when there is nothing to think about and rest is the greatest luxury on earth.

Such an interlude was one at the end of the McAree Portage, where I sat and idly scuffed the moss with the toe of my boot. I felt something hard and, thinking it might be a root, kicked it loose. To my surprise, it was an old knife, heavily rusted, with the horn handle partly gone. I scraped off the rust and there was the mark IXL, one of the trade knives carried by Indians and voyageurs. Dropped perhaps during a meal or after skinning a beaver, there it had lain until I kicked it free. That knife is now in the cabin, a reminder to me not only of the days of the fur trade but of the delight of a resting-place on the portage from McAree to the island-studded reaches of Lac la Croix.

No one in the Quetico-Superior country has arrived, however, until he has made the Kashapiwi Portage, a mile of the most rugged terrain along the border. It starts from Yum Yum Lake and is fairly level at first, then goes down into a swampy beaver flowage where in the spring the water may be waist deep, and then over a high and mountainous ridge. The view from that ridge of the knifelike gash that is Kashapiwi and its high shores, with the realization that only those who are willing to take the punishment of that grueling trail may see it, is reward enough.

Some lakes have no portages between them because most travelers follow major routes. Between these routes, however, are waterways unknown and unexplored. An itinerant hunter or trapper may have worked his way into them, but a blazed trail without continual use grows swiftly back to brush and trees. Sometimes when exploring it is necessary to cut a trail into one of these waters off the known paths of travel, an experience modern canoeists may still enjoy. In the early days before aerial surveys and photographs, before dependable maps were even dreamed of, there were many blank spaces where the country was a challenge.

Years ago I was camped on Robinson Lake just north of the border, determined to explore the country toward the northwest. One day we pushed into a long bay and thought we were on the route to the lakes I had heard were there. At one point we lifted the canoe around a log that blocked our passage through a narrows into another lake, but found it was just a swampy bay of Robinson itself and that we would have to try again.

The following morning we climbed a high hill in the far east end of Dart Lake and then a tall pine that gave us a sweep of the country to the north. There, as I had hoped, was a single spot of blue nestled between the ridges. We spent the morning blazing a portage through a swamp and did not finish the carry until late afternoon. On the shore of our little spot of blue at last, we were thrilled because it was wild and unknown and we were on our way. Three deer stood in the shallows at the far end, spots of orange in the last level rays of the sun. A blue heron flapped lazily away, and signs of moose were along the shore. A rocky ledge loomed beyond the narrows. We would camp there if we could find a level spot and in the morning head for the north and the waters we now were sure lay before us.

We loaded in the packs and paddled out into deeper water, and a school of bass followed us unafraid. At the narrows a windfall blocked our way, so we beached the canoe and walked around it. Then suddenly I was overcome with a powerful sense of having been there before, and with good reason, for there in the sand was the clear sharp imprint of a boot. We looked at it in shocked and incredulous amazement just as Robinson Crusoe must have done when he saw the track of Friday on the sands of his lonely island. Then we knew the truth. That footprint was where I had stepped out the day before, and the channel was the one we had explored out of Robinson Lake. Neither of us said a word; we just carried the canoe around the log and paddled back to the campsite we had left with such high hopes that morning. We had made a complete circle, cut a portage that never again would be used by man, but all was not lost, for we had known the thrill of exploration and, until the final realization of our error, the excitement of seeing country for the first time.

But of all the portages I have known, the one I most often dream about when I am far from the canoe country is along a knifelike ledge of rock between two gorges on the Saganagons. On my first trip down that river I camped there on a tiny level shelf of rock on a night that was full of the thunder of rapids and falls on either side. That place made such an impression on my young mind it has become endowed with mystery and I have only to close my eyes to hear its music.

And there are many more, those that wind between the boles of great trees and those with far vistas from the highlands with their smooth glaciated rocks like pavements through the woods. There are short delightful ones, merely interludes between the paddling, and long hard ones from one watershed to another. But always they are gateways to adventure, meeting-places for voyageurs, punctuation marks between the long blue sentences of lakes across the maps.

CHAPTER 20

PAINTED ROCKS

INDIAN paintings are found on smooth cliff faces all over the Quetico-Superior area. Reddish brown in color and seldom large, they adorn the rocks along many major routes of travel as high as a man can reach from a canoe. These strange likenesses of animals and birds, of suns and moons, canoes and figures of symbolic meaning, are found from the Atlantic to the Pacific, as well as along the waterways of the Canadian Shield.

No one today knows when they were done, who the artists were, or what they mean. All we know is that the pigment used was a combination of fish oil or animal fat with one of the iron oxides common to the continent; that they are similar not only to the petroglyphs or rock carvings of our west, but to the prehistoric paintings and carvings in many other countries of the world. We can only wonder as to their meaning, but believe that, whatever they portray and wherever they are, they represent the first groping attempts of Stone Age man for the expression of his creative powers.

To realize the possibility that some of these pictographs might be close to the point was exciting. One morning when the water was sparkling and a tail wind holding from the west, we paddled to the place where we had heard they might be found. For years I had wanted to locate them, but had always gone off on longer expeditions to the north.

The shoreline toward the east was rugged, seemed to have few of the vertical cliffs of smooth rock faces rising from the water's edge where we had always found them before. Just as we were about to give up our search, we slipped in close to a high bush-covered slope, discovered there an open face of ledge hidden behind a clump of trees. Hopefully we pushed aside the branches, expecting the familiar figures, but all we saw was some iron staining partly obscured by lichen. Though we examined the entire cliff carefully, exploring every possibility, we found nothing even remotely resembling a pictograph. While we sat there in a canoe wondering where the paintings might be, a swift vision of those we had found in other places passed before me.

A month earlier I had been at the famous pictured rocks of Crooked Lake along the border, where the cliffs rise straight and sheer for a hundred feet or more. The rocks themselves are very beautiful there, colored by lichens and stained in long undulating ribbons of color by the iron formations above. The bands are gray and orange and black, with patterns of blues and greens, and when the water ripples, reflections of these ribbons of color extend below in a shimmering liquid curtain as though the cliffs had fanned out onto the surface. But even though the unusual beauty of the cliff itself has stopped travelers for centuries, it is the smooth face protected by an overhanging ledge that is of the most interest today. Here some forgotten race recorded in magic symbols its deeds of prowess and valor. Here are moose, pelicans, war canoes, a loon with a fish inside, a medicine man with horns on his head, a caribou that looks like an ibex from the Asiatic mainland.

One of the famous landmarks along the voyageurs' highway and known to thousands of travelers in the days of the fur trade, the paintings were never mentioned in the journals. Explorers spoke of the colors of the cliff and called it the Rock of Arrows because at one time the great crack which cuts diagonally across it was full of feathered shafts. The cliff was a meeting-place for voyageurs from Lake Superior

on their way to the far northwest and those who were returning from Athabasca and the Mackenzie. The diaries often
mention the Rock of Arrows, but never a word about the
finest examples of pictograph art in the area.

Alexander Mackenzie wrote in 1801:

> *Within three miles of the last portage into Lac la Croch
> [Crooked Lake] is a remarkable rock with a smooth face,
> but split and cracked in different parts which hang over
> the water. Into one of the horizontal chasms a great num-
> ber of arrows have been shot, which is said to be done by
> a war party of the Nadawasis or Sioux who had done
> much mischief in this country and left these weapons as
> a warning to the Chebois or natives, that notwithstanding
> its lakes, rivers and rocks, it was not inaccessible to their
> enemies.*

Alexander Henry the Younger mentioned the rock in one
of his journals in 1800:

> *Thence we went down several ugly rapids . . . por-
> taged 100 paces over a rock to Lac la Croch. At the
> Rock of Arrows, we met nine canoes loaded with Atha-
> basca packs. At sunset we came to Portage de Rideau
> [Curtain Falls] where we stopped for the night.*

Almost a quarter of a century later, in 1823, Dr. J. J.
Bigsbee described the rock:

> *We next came to a narrows of still water, the entrance
> in fact of Lake Croche about twenty miles long. This*

*narrows is walled by high precipices of shattered granite,
beautifully striped by broad bands of white, yellow, red,
green and black stains. Until lately the arrows shot by
the Sioux during a conflict at this spot might be seen
sticking in the clefts of the rock.*

But not a word about the Indian paintings on the cliffs,
only mention of the war party and rendezvous with other
expeditions. If they had only known that the Indian paintings
were of far greater significance, their diaries would have been
full of awe and wonderment. We can only conclude that
pictographs were so common along their entire route of
travel from Montreal that they were not considered important enough to be mentioned. It has been suggested they
might have been done after the days of the fur trade were
past, but if that were so, modern Indians would surely understand their meaning and know what tribes had done them.

The area surrounding the point is rich in such paintings. To
the north in a bay of Darkey Lake are some of the finest, so
clear and sharp and unfaded they might have been made in
recent times. I paddled by them a year ago and was horrified
to find a fringe of protecting birch was gone and the paintings
fully exposed to the sun for the first time in my memory.
Beavers were the vandals, had cut the trees for food and
had stored the topmost branches in the water around a newly
built lodge near by. These paintings show a hunting expedition, a moose cow and calf with footprints on either side,

a great sea serpent with a horned head surrounded by hunters in canoes.

On Hegman Lake a few miles to the northeast is another splendid group showing a bull moose with wide branching antlers, as well done as though a modern artist had conceived it. A pelican stands to one side and on the other a mountain lion with a long curving tail.

To the north on Lac la Croix are cliffs where men of the past dipped their hands into pigment and pressed them against the wall. Some of the imprints are very large, others child-like in size. Such hand paintings also occur in the caves of the Dordogne in France and in Spain. The privilege of leaving such a mark may have been a reward for valor or a pledge of loyalty. No one will ever know.

Paintings are found on the Kawishiwi and Isabella rivers to the south, and no doubt hidden surfaces will be discovered for years to come as the country becomes better known.

On an expedition down the Churchill River in upper Manitoba and Saskatchewan I found them all along the route of travel. Though a thousand miles or more to the north-west of the Quetico-Superior, in the land of the Woodland Crees, they were identical with the rest. But in addition there was a figure I had seen nowhere else and one whose meanings some of the older Indians still understood. These were the Mannegishi, who, according to legend, are little people with round heads and no noses who live with only one purpose: to play jokes on travelers. The little creatures have long spidery legs, arms with six-fingered hands, and live between rocks in the rapids. When a canoe comes hurtling down, their greatest delight is to grasp the ends of paddles, and if the craft tips over, their shrieks of joy can be heard above the thunder of the water. If anything strange or unaccountable happens anywhere in the land of the Crees, it is the Mannegishi who are responsible.

Here at last were Indians who knew something of the meaning of the rock-paintings. Though none knew who did them and many scoffed at their authenticity, the story had survived. At one portage, until recent times, Indians still left offerings of food, tobacco, or trinkets at a rock where the Mannegishi were painted, in order to ensure safe passage through the rapids below. If these little figures meant something to the Crees, the others must have had significance as well.

Here again along the far reaches of the Churchill was evidence of the creative impulse in Stone Age man that had produced the pictographs not only on this continent but all over the world. Though colors might vary, they were generally composed of mixtures of the different oxides of iron with animal fats, yellow from the ocher, black from the manganese, reds and browns from limonites and hematites. Iron-bearing rock is a common mineral, and when powdered and mixed with any fat it becomes a durable pigment that, where protected from the elements, can survive for centuries with little change in brilliance.

Through such primitive painting it has been possible to

trace the development of man's attempt to portray not only the life around him but his dreams and fears. From the first scratchings on the rock walls of caves to rude outlines of forms and the final artistic and colorful figures of animals with which he was familiar is the story of his progress. Even more significant than the beauty and perfection of these ancient paintings of the Ice Age was the emergence thousands of years before the oldest civilizations of the use of line and suggestion to portray the world of magic and spirit and hidden meaning.

According to prehistorians, some thirty thousand years passed before the primitive markings on walls of rock developed into naturalistic painting. Another twenty thousand years later appeared the first attempts at expressionism, and only during the last five thousand the hieroglyphic symbols that preceded the written alphabets of western civilization.

The pictographs I had found along the canoe routes to the north were as important as any in the world. Their actual age did not matter. They may have been done only a few centuries ago or belong to the post-Ice Age. Whatever their final designation in the research of moderns, we know that together with all the other surviving examples of prehistoric art, they are among the most ancient records of mankind, tell of the eons when man pondered his environment while the awareness slowly came upon him that the dreams, the longings and fears that had haunted his nebulous past could be translated into forms of meaning and permanence.

No one will ever know exactly with what meaning primitive man endowed his artistic creations, but to us they are filled with magic and spirit. They may have been symbols from which spells went forth to influence hunting, fertility and success in his various ventures. They might well indicate the first vague glimmerings of the mighty concept of immortality and the dawning of the realization that after death he and his kind would dwell in the vast vault of the unknown. Whatever their interpretation, they marked the period during which Stone Age man emerged from the dark abyss of his past into the world of mind and soul.

The waves were higher now, still coming out of the west. We were forced to dodge behind islands and points in order to make any headway at all. Once we sought shelter back of a sharp ledge and there found another face of rock, but again no pictographs, only a mass of green and black lichen covering the surface, the *"tripe de roche"* of the voyageurs. That ledge made me wonder what might eventually be the fate of all the paintings in the north. Far more of a threat than vandals who might chip the pigment off the rocks is the slow and steady encroachment of lichens. Some of the paintings I knew are already becoming vague, and once they are covered, no one will ever find them again.

Across the channel on the way back to the point, the whitecaps were rolling and spray dashed high against the rocks. We fought them all the way across, rounded the headland at last and dashed into the shelter of the bay. After beaching the canoe, we started a fire, and as we sat there and listened to the roaring of the gale through the tops of the trees, we wondered where the hidden paintings might be, what secret cliffs along those many miles of shoreline primitive artists might have chosen for their work.

There was much to explore, but we would never rest until we had found them, for these Indian paintings are of tremendous significance. Not only are they evidence of man's growth in mind and spirit, but also of a force that, over the millennia, has resulted in all cultural development, art and music and literature, inventions, science, and the entire fabric of the civilization he has built. From such humble beginnings came all of this. The paintings at the Rock of Arrows, on Lac la Croix and Darkey Lake, and everywhere in the world are symbols of this eternal striving, shrines to the mind of man. Here was something worth finding, a challenge we could not ignore.

CHAPTER 21

GLACIAL STRIAE

J ust below the water line at the north end of the point are parallel scratches on the smooth surface of the ledge. Their direction is plain, as it is all over the north: roughly northeast to southwest. They are the marks of glaciers which once covered most of the northern part of the continent. I have seen them on ice-smoothed

174

islands and points all over the Canadian Shield, as fresh and distinct as if they were made just a few years ago. Some are narrow and deep as though a giant lathe had gouged the surface of the rock, some wide and shallow where a huge round boulder did the cutting, some merely the scratches of gravel like those before me, but all in the same general direction, indicating the steady advance of the glacial front from north to south.

Above the water line, weathering had rubbed the marks out long ago, and lichens and caribou moss had grown over them, but under the water they are sharp and clear.The end of the point is polished smooth, round and gently sloping to the water. The little knob where we watch the moonrise is merely a higher extension of the point itself, a place that, due to extra hardness perhaps, forced the ice to ride high. Near the shore and close to the striations are several smoothly gouged depressions which look like the sides of kettle holes, where the surface might have been worn by a turning stone imprisoned in the basin beneath some falls of a glacial stream.

All this began a million years ago, when the coolness of the climate gradually increased, until at last the accumulation of snow in the highlands of Labrador and in the region of Hudson Bay began to form extensive areas of ice. Even today the center of the Greenland ice-cap is eight thousand feet in thickness and there is reason to believe bygone centers of glacier formation spread for hundreds of miles in all directions. This advance of the ice sheets over vast sections of

North America was the most spectacular event of the Pleistocene epoch on the continent. During each advance glacial ice rode over the Quetico-Superior country and far to the south.

Glacial periods were separated by long intervals of warmer climate during which the great masses of ice melted and dropped their loads of morainic debris. The last advance began its retreat some ten to eleven thousand years ago, moved as far south as Missouri, northeast Kansas and central Iowa. Each of the four major glaciers that moved over this terrain continued in motion for many thousands of years, always moving forward, scouring the soil off the rocks, gouging like huge rasps the surface of the earth, shoving all before it and underneath, changing the entire topography and destroying life.

Those marks beneath the water line on the point were left there that long ago. When the glaciers had finished their work, the north country, with the exception of its vegetation, looked much as it does today. It has taken all this time to form the ten inches of soil and humus that lie on the mainland, all this time for the naked rocks to grow the forests, the lichens and mosses and flowering plants that now provide its cover. After the ice had gone there was little humus, only crushed rock and sand and gravel. All that exists now is the result of slow accumulation of decay since then. But some areas still have no soil, lie as stark and bare as the rains and snows and fires can make them; I have never seen them from the air without thinking that here are the bare bones of the continent showing through.

When an ice mass ground forward, trees and vegetation were engulfed and the environment changed for all living things in its path. Because of the slowness of the advance, the northern coniferous forests actually seemed to move southward ahead of the flow and then with the melting followed its receding forefront back again the way they had come. Records indicate that at one time the northern conifers were found as far south as Iowa, and in glacial deposits are the remains of elk and reindeer, bison and musk ox, even the hairy mammoth, which followed the ice. Man, being dependent on these forms of life for food, no doubt migrated with the rest.

At the present time, we are in an interglacial period and enjoying an interval of moderate climate which might well last a hundred thousand years. It might mark the end of the great Ice Age, or the beginning of a new one, but if we are to judge by the melting of the arctic ice today, the world will be assured of an equable climate for a long time to come.

Some years ago I accompanied the famous geologist Dr. Wallace Atwood on an aerial glaciological survey of the Quetico-Superior country. We were familiar with the ground, knew the places where striations could be found and all the glacial gougings over the entire area. We wanted to see what had happened to the old pre-glacial stream patterns, to find out if any remnants were left of the ancient dendritic drainage systems which carried the wreckage of the Laurentians toward the plains of the south. We also wanted a bird's-eye view of the flow of the ice itself, to see striations on a gigantic scale, to sense—if we could, ten thousand years after it had happened—the drama of the last invasion. We knew if we flew high enough, we could see more at a glance than any ground exploration could possibly tell us.

At thousands of feet on a clear sunny day, the Quetico-Superior lay below us, the stippled blues and greens of the wilderness canoe country, such myriads of potholes and lakes and connecting streams it seemed as though most of it were water. But then as we looked close between the network of waterways, we saw the roots of the Laurentians where once great rock masses, from five to ten miles in thickness, had been folded and broken and crushed to rear the once majestic ranges and then eroded, as all mountains eventually are, to make the sandstones and shales that mantle much of the continent's interior. What lay below us now were the ancient roots of those mountains, worn almost to sea level but still rugged enough to have cliffs and canyons and hills.

It was over this complex of tortured rock that the great ice sheets advanced, each one gouging and polishing and erasing the scars of the ones preceding it. In the days before the glacial age there had been regular drainage patterns, major river valleys with tributaries running into them as the branches of a tree run into its trunk, valleys carved by the streams themselves. But the old familiar patterns of drainage were nowhere to be seen, and the streams that now existed appeared to be flowing along the floors of lake basins and depressions gouged by the ice. A tiny rivulet might begin in a broad open valley, then plunge suddenly into a narrow rocky gorge. A large river might occupy a course too small for its volume and then run in the wrong direction. The white lacework of rapids held the chains of lakes together, young streams all of them and at many different levels. This was the disarranged drainage pattern typical of the Canadian Shield, of Finland, Siberia and all of northwest Europe where ice conditions had been the same.

We had been so intent on studying the confused network of waterways that we had almost forgotten the general arrangement of the lakes themselves. There they lay in concentric patterns like the huge striations they actually are, lying parallel one to the other, sometimes in slightly curving groups showing how the ice had swerved from its true direction and been shunted to east or west to conform to the terrain. It was as though a many-fingered hand had scraped its path to the south. But some of the lakes, like the Kasha-piwi chain, were different from the rest. They followed old fault lines as straight as though they had been laid out with surveyors' instruments, lines sometimes almost parallel to the flow of ice, then again at right angles cutting directly across the striations and adding still more confusion to the tangle already there.

It is hard to believe that the ice was heavy enough to cut into the rock itself, but the evidence is indisputable. Thousands of feet have tremendous weight, and with the boulders in its base it cut through the native greenstone, granite, and basalt as though they were putty. Some of the depressions are small, only a few acres in extent, but others cover thirty to forty square miles.

But the cutting and polishing of the ice was only a small part of its total effect. The enormous mass of debris shoved before it and on either side and underneath, the boulders and gravel, the sand and crushed rock gathered in a thousand miles of its advance, played a major part in the shaping of the new topography. When the ice melted, these masses of material were left as lateral moraines on either side, as terminals at the forefront, as ground morainic till underneath with the winding eskers that outlined the beds of glacial rivers. When the melting occurred, these masses of debris dammed the waters, imprisoned them in countless pockets and depressions, cut them off in thousands of ice-formed basins, some high, some low, left a vast confusion of disconnected waters that had no place to go.

Today, after thousands of years of erosion, many of the higher lakes have trickled through their morainic dams to join waters down below. Here are the streams beside many of the portages flowing over the sand and gravel of the old depositions.

At the end of the glacial period the streams were very immature, had not yet cut their channels or confined themselves to any particular direction or flow, but in time the new divides, somewhat influenced by the old Laurentian hills, became established through the equalization of erosion. These divides shunted the water into Lake Superior and eventually to the Atlantic, from the border lakes into the Rainy Lake system emptying into the waters of Hudson Bay, from the edge of the Shield into the Mississippi and the Gulf of Mexico. The Quetico-Superior region can well be called the ridgepole of the continent because from its heights the waters run in three directions.

I walked along the shores, and wherever the rock was smooth I found the glacial striae. I could picture the great mass of ice coming from the north, moving only a few feet each year, digging out the bed of Burntside Lake, riding over hard resistant peaks of old hills and leaving them as islands across the channel. I thought of the great erratic boulder on its narrow spit of rock with the Norways growing around it, of the rows of such boulders on glaciated shelves of rock all through the area. One stood before the cabin, a block of greenstone that might have come from a cliff hundreds of miles to the north, another just below of red granite whose source I do not know.

To the south are the ancient beaches of glacial Lake Duluth that preceded Lake Superior, to the west the gravel shorelines of Lake Agassiz, the greatest fresh-water lake the continent has ever known. Though now a fertile farming land, those beaches mark the ancient shorelines. Even the little beach in the bay of Listening Point is glacial sand washed up from the bottom by the winds of centuries.

All about me in the fifteen thousand square miles of the Quetico-Superior is a beauty that owes its existence to the ice.

Without its scouring the rocks would be rough and the campsites difficult to find. Without its melting and the morainic dams the lakes might be far apart or nonexistent and the portages long. The falls and rapids of its new rivers plunging over rocky ledges would not be here unless the ancient erosion patterns had been disturbed. The mosses and the lichens that thrive in this water-drenched land, the Norways and the white pines that give it artistry might be missing had the glaciers not been here. This is a land to love, a land of poetry, cleanness and beauty, where men may always refresh their spirits and find release.

CHAPTER 22

FALLING LEAF

I T WAS a bright and sparkling
morning in late August with just enough hint of frost in the
air to make one question the permanence of summer. A
blue jay screamed the hard clarion notes of coming fall, and
in that sound was the promise of change.

I stood beside the big boulder on top of the point. Beyond

183

it and silhouetted against the blue of the north channel was a large-toothed aspen. A small scraggly tree, it was sparse of leaves and branches and its roots went into a crevice of the rock. Standing there alone, it was like a Japanese painting in its stark simplicity. If the blue jay was right, it would be one of the first to turn, would change while the shores were still massed with green. Unconsciously I looked toward the top, and, to my surprise, the leaves seemed tinged with a faint glow. At the very top a single leaf danced and turned in a sudden breeze, then separated itself from the branch and whirled in slow fluttering circles down to where I stood. I picked it up, twirled it between my fingers, observed the prominent veining, the great even scallops along its edges, and the end of its stem, where growing cellulose had severed it from its holdfast.

The base of the leaf was yellowish green, but along the sides and tip it was tinted with peach and rose—and this only the end of August! I looked at that first color as though I had never seen such beauty before that moment. It was hard to realize that the warmth now showing through had been there all the time, hidden by green chlorophyll until fading sunshine and growing cold had stopped its production. In that fallen leaf was the story of the season's advance, an indicator of shortening days and lengthening nights.

Summer comes slowly in the north, is never fully here until the end of June, and sometimes, when June is rainy and cold, it actually seems to start in July. But to have the change begin before summer has really settled down and the leaves grown to maturity is a shock when you have waited for it and dreamed about it since the snows disappeared and rivers ran free of ice.

I remembered a flash of red I had seen two weeks before on the south shore of the lake. It had not impressed me then, for the time was mid-August and it could not possibly be a warning. Perhaps, I reasoned, a beaver had gnawed the bark, cutting the flow of sap, or exploring roots had found a dry crevice in the rocks and the tip, being starved for food and moisture, had gone into early flame. Surely it could be nothing else, for the days were still balmy and the nights as well, and the water had barely warmed to the point where swimming was no longer an ordeal. But now I knew that the crimson flag against the solid green of the hillside had responded exactly as the leaf of the aspen had done; that, whatever the combination of circumstances, waning sunlight had hastened the change.

I tucked the lone leaf carefully into my wallet. It would remind me to be aware while summer was slipping away. The leaves in the top of the little tree shuddered suddenly in a breeze, then danced and pirouetted as only aspen leaves can. Another floated down and rested its color on a bed of bright-green moss behind the boulder.

A few days later in the end of a swampy bay on the Basswood River I found a stand of ash turning to lemon yellow after a bare three months of growth. No wonder they mature slowly with three months of green and nine of bareness standing in the cold acid medium of a bog.

That same day I found a bright-red leaf of wild geranium laced flatly against a ledge of greenstone. Beside it was a cluster of pink corydalis still in bloom and just beyond the sky blue of a single long-stemmed aster. Under the trees the bracken had changed to russet and bronze, and when I looked closely I found the entire forest floor moving slowly into color, a dwarf honeysuckle in red and a mountain maple shifting to the peach and rose that would brighten thickets until all the leaves were on the ground.

On the Robinson River we paddled to a flat ledge where the water races down toward Moose Bay of Crooked Lake. Above the break a mat of poison ivy growing in a crevice had turned, each stem and leaf shouting "Danger—do not touch!" On an old burn just beyond, a thousand asters were in bloom and goldenrod as well, the first of the blues and golds of Indian summer before the storms came down.

By the middle of September, maples were flaming along all the roadsides from Lake Superior to the border. Mountain-ash berries hung in crimson clusters, and along the rivers the rice had turned from light green to yellow. Ducks were on the move, and on the Bear Island, the Burntside, and the Stony the whisper of wings could be heard at dusk.

Now were the days of color and of finding the places where it was best, for time does not wait in the north and a gale could change it swiftly overnight. Nothing more important now than reveling in shifting panoramas, exploring scenes remembered vaguely from the past, surcharging minds and spirits with color and warmth against the coming white and cold. There were many places to go, each one different, places that somehow had poetry of their own and, while part of the changing scene, stood out and said: "Enjoy me while you can."

One such place was in the darkness of the pines. We found it one day when the gloom was sprinkled with flecks of dusty rose and Chinese red, flecks that seemed to be floating and held in suspension. In places they were almost blown together and continuous, but even so there was a lightness and evanescence against the black-green of the pines that is never found where the sun shines directly on the trees. As we stood there the black tracery of branches gradually disappeared and we saw what an artist sees in his painting, flecks of color and the illusion of stems without their actual portrayal.

This was the prelude, the elfin flutes and almost inaudible strings that set the tone for the bold crescendos of blue and gold and red to come. Then with the ground as colorful as the trees themselves, with the atmosphere charged with power, it would be hard to remember when the first faint hints of change drifted into the woods and the somberness was dusted with floating bits of light.

I wondered as I stood there beside a great pine looking at the ephemeral drifts, the black tracery of branches, looking through them and their infinite variations, if this weren't the best of all, but I knew that here was only one muted note, that without the rest the symphony would not be complete. But even as I stood there I was conscious of deepening color far beyond the pines and along the crest of a ridge, and knew that while the delicacy and evanescence was there, boldness was beginning to show.

I tried to hold for a little while the beauty before me, the sense of floating color and the artistry of flame against the dark, knowing it was part of the smells and sounds and rememberings of the past. Nothing could possibly be lovelier, or so I believed, forgetting that each year I had thought the same. I tried to think of the coming hush with the leaves on the ground and all the color drained from the hills, the somber browns and greens waiting for the snow, but somehow all I could see was what was before me, a moment like a poem long remembered in the days to come.

One night we unrolled our sleeping-bags under a full moon beneath a maple that had turned to gold, lay there and watched the light streaming through. The ground was silver and gold and the air as well. We were bathed in the glow, became part of it, and drifted off to sleep. Several times we awakened, watched the play of light above until drowsiness claimed us again.

The morning sun picked out the topmost branches glistening with frost. A single branch burst into flame, as did a cluster of brown cones in the top of a pine. We lay there and watched the lazy spiraling down of leaves. I touched the trunk of a near-by sapling and a cascade of frosted color filtered down upon our bags. Behind us crimson sumacs fringing a little glade were dusted with silver.

By mid-October the leaves were falling fast and the shore-lines turning everywhere. The little bay with its cedar and aspen had changed with the rest, and islands and the mainland were solid gold as far as I could see. Only in a few places was there any touch of red, on the hilltops where the scrub oaks still held their leaves and in protected bays where winds could not reach.

But along the roadsides and underneath the trees now appeared a display that until then had been hidden from view. Cherries, mountain maple, Juneberry, honeysuckle, and hazel all had turned to shades of red and gold. Blueberry and bearberry beneath the pines were now a carpet of crimson. Together with the fallen leaves, they made the entire forest floor a tapestry of color even richer and more varied than the trees had been. Now for the first time one could look through the woods and far into them with vistas that seemed to stretch on endlessly into more and more color.

Even the bogs began to turn from their summer's green and brown to tones of copper, each muskeg a soft carpet, the heathers blending together to complement the brilliant shrubs that hemmed them close.

The rice beds in rivers and swampy bays were yellow against the blue. Portages were deep in leaves, for all the glory that had been was on the ground. For a month the color had been almost more than could be borne. Senses had been surfeited by overwhelming beauty. Now at last the somberness could come and eyes could rest and minds as well.

Early in November I stood by the boulder where I had watched the first falling leaf come down. They were all gone now and the little large-toothed aspen stood stark and bare against the sky. The hush was already upon the land and a softness that had not been there before. Rains had come and the ground had lost its glow and was turning brown, smelled of dampness and of coming mold. Already those brilliant leaves were turning into duff and soon would be part of the black humus underneath, lending their richness to the earth, and from them would come the color of autumns in the future.

The leaf I had pressed six weeks before, though now dry and sere, still had its shades of peach and rose, was almost as beautiful as when it had fluttered down before me. It reminded me of those drifting flecks of color in the deep pines one misty morning, of flaming roadsides clear to Lake Superior, of a night when the moon was full and we lay under a maple drenched in its golden light. In that little leaf was all the poetry of fall, the first soft prelude of the symphony just finished. The cycle was complete once more. Now the snows could come.

CHAPTER 23

COCK OF THE WOODS

W E WERE down at the beach
starting a fire for tea. It was a soft misty sort of day in early
November. As yet there was no snow, and the ground was
sodden with rain. Not a leaf remained of the color of October, but the grasses along the water's edge were golden and
brown. A windrow of pine needles had washed up at the

edge of the sand, the shedding from the pines all along the west shore, and from the islands we could see across the open reaches of the lake. They had come to rest in this little bay as they had for thousands of autumns in the past.

All sounds were muted. The air lay like a cushion over the grass and the trees and the slow swell that moved rythmically into the bay. I stood there and listened and felt as though all the world were in slow motion and that I must not hurry or make a sound that might disturb it.

It was while fanning to life the first little flame in the damp tinder that I saw a movement at the base of a dead aspen some thirty feet back from the shore. It was a huge bird, red and black and white, so startlingly colored and so large I could scarcely believe my eyes. Never before had I been so close to a pileated woodpecker, the cock of the woods of the north.

Time and again I had seen one in flight and had heard countless times the sharp staccato hammering from some high dry stub, but only a flash of black and white and a hint of the scarlet topknot as the bird flew across some opening and then the distant hammering once more.

Now one of the great birds was almost within reach. I forgot the fire, barely breathed for fear it would fly away. The topknot at that range was a far more brilliant red than I had imagined. The back, shiny black with a white bar reaching from the bill to the base of the wings, the crimson streak beneath the eye, indicated that this was a male in full plumage.

I had nothing to fear, for the woodpecker kept on with its steady methodical chipping away of the soft white decay at the base of the aspen stub in search of ants and larvae and wood-boring beetles. Suddenly it moved behind the stub and was out of sight. There was little sound, for the wood was soft and spongy with decay, sharp contrast to the hard brazen tattoos I had heard from the bone-dry pines of the past.

The fire began to burn with a crackle, and a little plume of smoke mounted straight toward the sky. I filled the teapot carefully and hung it on its stick to boil, and all the while cock of the woods kept on with its work. Once in a while, as it moved part way around, I would see the black or white or crimson, but just a hint and then it would go back again. It must have sensed the disturbance at the beach and my careful movements because it continued out of sight on the far side of the stub.

According to Thomas Roberts in *Birds of Minnesota*, "The pileated is a giant among woodpeckers and with a single exception, the rare ivory-billed woodpecker of the south, is the largest in North America. It weighs ten ounces or over while the little downy barely reaches an ounce. It is as large as a crow and nearly as black but adorned with a flaming scarlet crest and showing in flight, great white patches on the wings."

The bird now moved to my side of the stub and suddenly saw me, gave a startled squawk, and flew to its top. There it regarded me and the fire and the smoke with wide-eyed alarm.

Then off it went, it's *wicker-wicker-wicker* shattering the silence of the point. I watched its undulating flight through the trees until it disappeared over the ridge and then I heard the loud staccato once more, this time from a dead pine, like a pneumatic drill reverberating against its brittle hardness.

As I watched the teapot come to a boil, I thought of the many other times I had tried to get close enough to a pileated to really study it, of the time years ago on a canoe trip with a famed ornithologist when we had looked for weeks without being fortunate enough to see one. What wouldn't he have given for the view I had just had?

On that trip, while carrying the canoe across a portage, I had seen one sitting on a stub near the water's edge. I stopped dead in my tracks without changing the position of the canoe and waited for my friend to come along with the packs. I waited and waited while the canoe got heavier and heavier, and still he did not come. I must have stood there all of ten minutes while my arms turned slowly to jelly and my legs as well and the shoulder straps of the pack cut into my breathing.

Finally the brush cracked behind me and I hoped the ornithologist would realize in time the meaning of my sacrifice. Then, to my horror, a handful of gravel rained over the canoe. The bird flew off with a squawk of terror clear across a tamarack bog into a patch of dark timber on the other side of the bay. I dropped the canoe into the water just beside the stub, stood there for a moment breathing heavily.

I did not have to explain, and when I saw the woebegone expression on the face of my friend I had not the heart to berate him.

For almost a month we had trailed the bird, followed its hammering over valleys and muskegs all over the Quetico. Each time we would hear one or catch even a glimpse of its erratic flight, we would go ashore and take its trail. I thought of the miles of scrambling over the windfalls in choked canyons, wading knee deep in soft muskegs, climbing cliffs, stalking silently through stands of big timber, always on the watch, and the long circuitous trails back to the canoe with oftentimes nothing to show but the memory of its call or a tantalizing glimpse. To have one actually cornered and the triumphant moment destroyed by a handful of gravel was surely the irony of fate.

My friend confessed that he had been watching a field sparrow feeding its young in a bush right beside the portage, and when he had finally caught up to me standing there with the canoe on my back, the temptation for a little fun was too great.

As I sat there by the fire that morning I wished my friend had been with me, for this would have taken the sting out of that episode on the portage, would have been compensation for all the searching we had done.

As yet I had not found the nest of this pair of pileated woodpeckers. Usually in a dead stub some twenty to sixty feet above the ground, they occupy a hole that has been chiseled out of the solid wood in a way that no other bird can manage. In this part of the north they usually nest in May or June, lay from three to five eggs, and bring out their young after eighteen days of incubation. I knew that somewhere within the area of the point I would find the nest. It would take much waiting and watching and listening, but eventually I would find it, of that I was sure. With all the old dead aspen, their soft wood full of food, Listening Point was a pileated paradise, and as far as I was concerned it always would be. If dead aspen are important to woodpeckers, then they are important to me.

No so-called "forest improvement" would ever take place here, no elimination of breeding-places for ants and beetles and insects on the supposition they might be a hazard to living trees. The natural ecological balance would be preserved, and with the dead and decaying trees and their vital contribution to the survival of the species dependent upon them, the entire forest would benefit and thrive. To me and the pileated woodpecker no forest had character that was trimmed and manicured.

Cock of the woods, log cock, pileated woodpecker, whatever its name, has a character of its own and contributes to the meaning of any area where it is found. Typifying the old wilderness before it was disturbed by man, in its way it is just as fragile. Like all forms of life that have reached stability and have maintained a position of pre-eminence for a long period of time, it is more easily influenced by changes than lesser types. Developed areas may have their little birds and small mammals but seldom the larger forms of life. These species, the peaks of their particular ecological pyramids, have reached pinnacles of dominance only in close correlation with climax vegetational types over a long period of time. When the old environments are changed, they are the first to go— the eagles, the wolves, the mountain lions and moose. Man the earth-mover who manages terrain with the thought that what is good for him must be good for all living things, man who cannot tolerate any form of life that he feels might threaten his survival, does not realize that when he destroys an old and stable balance he unwittingly destroys himself. If he only knew it, he is as dependent on dead stubs as the pileated woodpeckers themselves.

In the early days the cock of the woods was very common, but with the advent of logging and the inevitable aftermath of fires, dead stubs disappeared over large areas. But now the species is coming back and growing plentiful once more, has even been reported near settled areas where the old trees have been allowed to stand. There would always be the lesser types on the point, the diminutive downy, the sapsucker, and the hairy. These I could take for granted, and I enjoyed them none the less, but it was the pileated that really put the stamp of wildness on the area.

The big-game hunting season was just a week away, and I decided to put up a few NO HUNTING signs not only to save the deer in the cedar swamp back of the beach, but the pileated woodpeckers as well. When I thought of the one I had seen that morning and what a target it would make for some sharpshooter, I decided to act quickly. Its loss would be as tragic to me as the big buck which had yarded there the winter before. In a sense it was as much the top of its pyramid as the buck itself, or the timber wolves that still ranged the Quetico-Superior country. Down through the ages its position had been maintained. All the lesser types of insectivorous birds were part of it, but minor parts in its base. There was only room for one on top.

And, like all pinnacles, it was a tenuous position to hold, for the habitat had become specialized, food chains narrowed, nesting requirements definitely set. If any one of these vital factors were disturbed or any of the minor species supporting the pyramid's base strengthened, the exalted place that until then had been held only by sufferance would no longer be secure. One crack in the armor of the king and he might fall, one shift in any of the blocks supporting the structure beneath him and his throne would shake.

Ceophiloes pileatus abieticola Bangs, one of the twenty-two species of the Picidae in America, the cock of the woods wore its regal topknot as a true monarch should, with dignity and unconscious aplomb, sure of its position and entitled to its place in the ecological pattern of the region. The great bird did not know how tenuous its position. Should a great wind blow up some day and topple the dead stubs, a fire come, or too much artificial development adjacent to the point, it would be forced to flee and find a kingdom elsewhere.

I could hear the bird hammering away back in the woods. It was on a hard stub now, because the staccato was loud and clear. It would soon give up such heartbreaking work and return to the aspen back at the beach, and I had not long to wait. Of a sudden there was a flash of black and white, and there it was again at the base of the same tree it had abandoned a short time before. Again I had a perfect vantage place, could see the big chips fly as it searched for the carpenter ants and grubs it would find there. Round and round it went, drilling one great hole after the other until the ground was white with chiseled wood. Then it was off once more, back into the timber from which it had come, back to the nesting-area I must soon find.

Wicker-wicker-wicker—the cock of the woods was announcing to all who would hear that it was the woodpecker king of Listening Point.

CHAPTER 24

THE PADDLE

I T WAS good to sit there in front of the fire whittling the new paddle. It was elemental work, like shaping a spear or a bow, and when I smoothed the blade and handle I felt nothing could be more vital or important. The very act of shaping it set up a deep-seated chain of subconscious reactions that were satisfying, basic, and primitive.

THE PADDLE

It was still a little heavy where the blade fanned out, so I scraped one side and then the other, not enough to weaken it, just what was necessary to bring out the natural resiliency of the wood. A paddle must be elastic, have none of the deadness of too much fiber, must bend when it feels the water. Like a bow, it must be alive, but not so much alive it might break under the strain. There is a fine point beyond which you cannot go, and only one who has used a paddle long can tell when it is reached.

At last it seemed right, so I stood and tested it by placing its point against the floor and bending it with my weight. Just so would it feel the weight of my arm against the solidity of the water. It was close, very close, but not quite right, and I scraped and polished a little more. Another testing and I felt I had reached the exact balance and spring I wanted.

The blade itself needed trimming along the edges so when it knifed the water there would be no splash, no clumsy noise of retrieving, only a smooth and quiet ripple when it entered and when it left.

The upper end for the hand was honed to the point where my fingers had just enough to grasp and nothing more; partly round, partly square, a shape a hand would appreciate, no crowding of the fingers, no rubbing of its top into the palm, just a smooth and easy hold.

Now the paddle bent under my weight from any position I tried. I looked at the long smooth grain, not a single strand of which came out at any place. Those strands of fiber, channels for the flowing of the sap, ran as true down the length of the blade and into the handle itself as though they had grown for the very purpose I had in mind. It should rise to the challenge of all the good paddles I had ever known. Before it was through it would see great combers on the lakes, test its mettle against their surging power; it would know the shouting of the rapids as the canoe would bend and weave between the rocks.

The paddle is made of native ash from a tree that grew in a cold swamp and gathered its toughness from bitter springs and cold falls when even staying alive had been an effort. Its fineness of grain came from slowness of growth, some so fine it could barely be seen with the naked eye, evidence in those sections that life had been difficult. Into the new paddle went those qualities of texture and spirit that develop only under stress. In its aliveness and ability to take punishment and still survive against tremendous odds is the character and quality every canoeman looks for in his ideal blade.

Should I ever choose another, I shall go to some swamp where I know the struggle for existence has been just as hard. There I shall select a tree that in spite of everything has grown straight and true. Even so I will take only the straightest section, and when the wood is seasoned and ready I will split off a perfect piece, one that is true from end to end, for only through splitting is it possible to follow the grain. If the grain is straight, the paddle will have strength.

I have several old paddles that have been with me on many canoe trips, paddles without which any trip into the lake country would be inconceivable. Through long usage I know what they can do, that when the waves are high and the rapids fierce they will never fail me. Their handles have acquired a polish such as only use can give, not varnish or shellac, just a rubbing with oil or wax and the dark gleam and shine that countless hours of hard gripping can impart.

As I worked on the paddle, a gale was roaring outside; gusts of it came down the chimney and the coals glowed with their breath. In a sense it was like making a new friend, developing the first intimations of the loyalty and steadfastness of the future. By giving all I could now, I made sure that in the days to come it would be part of me and when my muscles strained, those long-fibered grains of ash would strain with me.

Paddles mean many things to those who know the hinterlands of the north. They are symbolic of a way of life and of the deep feeling of all voyageurs for the lake and river country they have known. Some time ago I received an envelope bordered in black, one of those old-fashioned conventional letters of mourning which today are no longer used. I glanced at the date and address, tried hard to remember from whom it might be. With hesitation and foreboding, I tore open the seal. Inside was a simple card edged in black and across the face of it the sketch of a broken paddle. In the lower corner was the name.

The significance of this death announcement struck me like a blow. The paddle was broken and my friend who had been with me down the wilderness lakes of the border regions on many trips had cached his outfit forever. That broken blade meant more than a thousand words of eulogy, said far more than words could ever convey. It told of the years that had gone into all of his expeditions, of campsites and waterways. In its simple tribute were memories of the rushing thunder of rapids, the crash of waves against cliffs, of nights when the loons called madly and mornings when the wilds were sparkling with dew. It told of comradeship and meetings on the trail, of long talks in front of campfires and the smell of them, of pine and muskeg and the song of whitethroats and hermit thrushes at dusk.

I know now, thinking of the broken paddle and what it really meant, that if a man in the course of time can so identify himself with a way of life that when he goes it is not just another passing, then he has achieved a lasting place in the memories of his fellows, a bond they will cherish forever. The broken paddle was an insignia forged in the wilds, of loyalty not only of men to each other but devotion to lasting and eternal things.

The paddle was about finished. I rubbed it down once more until it was satin to my touch, held it in the light of the fire and caught its golden gleam, tested it just to be sure, then stood it with the others to wait for spring.

Once I lost a paddle in the Pigeon River country above Grand Portage. It was one of the best, and I had placed it on top of a pack as I stepped ashore to reconnoiter a portage around a falls. When I came back to the canoe it was gone, and I knew what had happened. It had slipped into the current, plunged over the falls, and gone down through the rapids below them. For an hour I climbed over rocks in the gorge, explored every tangle of logs and windfalls on either bank, waded through the shallows down below, looked into every crevice, every place it might have lodged, but not a sign of it did I see. At last I climbed back to the canoe, unstrapped the spare paddle from the thwarts, and made the portage.

As I paddled down the lake, I had a sense of irretrievable loss. While the spare paddle was also sound and true, I did not know it, and days went by before it responded to my touch. But then I thought, if a paddle had to go, what better place could it end than in a roaring cataract where it would always hear the sounds of falling water which had become so much a part of it? For the day always comes to both men and the blades they use when decisions must be made as to where they must finally go.

And so it was with two old voyageurs who had made their last cruise together. They had spent a lifetime following the canoe trails of the north and, now past the conventional threescore and ten, realized they no longer could pack the canoe or slog across the portages. They hated to abandon their old weather-scarred canoe by storing it in some common place where it would slowly disintegrate away from the life it had known. They thought of burning it on some rocky point and letting the winds scatter the ashes, of sinking it in a rapids and letting it smash itself to bits in water it had known, but somehow all these things seemed wrong. Then came the brilliant thought of sawing it in two.

At first the solution seemed monstrous, the thought of putting a saw to the old gunwales and planking, of ripping through the canvas they had patched so many times. But the more they thought about it, the more logical it became. That ended the argument, and the craft was shipped to a town a thousand miles away, where one night at the end of a farewell dinner they drank a toast to their old canoe and sawed it in two.

Each voyageur took his half and stood it in a corner of a room where it would always be near. Shelves were fitted from each sawed-off base to its pointed end, and there a light was placed to shine on books, pictures, mementos, and the stuff of dreams. A paddle stands beside each bookcase now, a paddle that is dark and worn and scarred along its length. Whether ash or pine or spruce I do not know, but I do know it was chosen with care and used for a lifetime back in the bush.

The next morning I walked down the shore trail back into the swamp where the ash trees grew. It was wet there and the rocks were covered with moss, and during the summer it was shaded from the sun. The trees grew tall and straight, reaching for the light. Branches were sparse and far between, and there was no luxuriance of growth. I stood and looked them over, picked out a tall and straight one that someday I might use. Not yet—it could grow another year or two, build into its fiber even more of the strength it might need. I would fell it with care so it would not break, take the best part of it and store it where it would season and dry. The rest I would use in the fireplace, and some winter in the future, in the light of its flames, I might fashion another blade.

CHAPTER 25

THE SPAWNING

IT WAS February and the mercury was down to twenty below zero. We took off from the cabin when the moon was high and the surface of the lake glittering in its shine. The snow was firm, and the skis hissed as we pushed along. We did not stop to look at the moon or the stars, were only conscious of the fact we were moving through a brittle icy brightness, that the stars were close, almost close enough to touch. It was one of those winter nights in the north, one of those times close to midnight that come only when it is still and the moon is full.

We were off on important business, far more important than just going for a ski or enjoying the night. We were out to watch a spawning in midwinter, the mating of the eelpout, those brown eel-like deep-water fish that thrive in the cold depths of northern lakes. Seldom is one ever taken by hook and line except when they approach the shallows and the rivers to spawn, and seldom is one seen during the warm months of the year because of the deeps they frequent. Only in midwinter can their strange primordial mating be observed.

The river mouth was a mile away, opening like a lighted hallway into the black embankment of hills to the south. Beyond its far door were the rapids, a place where the frozen highway of the river was still alive and moving over the rocks. We stopped at the mouth and listened, and there was the same murmuring we had heard the first night we slept on the point, a murmuring that seemed to blend with our breathing and with the pounding of our hearts.

The eelpout need shallow water, moving water full of oxygen, gravel and sand to mix the sperm with the eggs, to keep them rolling over and over until the first cell divisions take place. As we skied up the narrowing river, its sound became plainer until there was a distinct and steady rushing.

The rocky shores drew together until they seemed to merge and become part of the woods. Then before us the rapids were suddenly loud and clear and we saw the glint of them in the moonlight. We stopped, unstrapped our skis and went into the trees, stayed quiet until the cold made us move. No vibration of the bank, no breaking twigs must announce our coming. Not until we were within ten feet of the rapids did we shine our lights and then saw such a sight as is seldom glimpsed by modern man, a struggling squirming mass of fish, the brownish snake-like bodies with their sinuous dorsal fins the full length of them twisted around each other, the entire contorted mass turning over and over, churning the water into froth.

Fascinated and oblivious of the cold, we stood and watched, for this was a scene out of the dim past, this mating, the rapids white with the concentration of eggs and milt and the foam from the threshing fish. Over and over rolled the mass, churning the precious eggs and sperms with the liveness of their bodies, whipping them together so there was no chance of an egg not meeting its exploring mate. Out of the depths they had come, swimming into the river and beneath the ice to reach this stretch of open water in the rapids and here in the night exchanging their offerings.

But why in February when the elements seemed against the success of any mating? Why not during the warm days of spring or in the summer or fall when all other species spawned? Why this terrible urge to leave the deeps in the dead of winter and spawn at night? Why does the whiskeyjack lay its eggs during the winter and hatch its young during the bitter days of March? Why does the horned owl do the same? Why do some species violate all traditional procedure? Such thoughts ran through my mind as we stood there and watched the eelpout spawn.

To answer, one must go back to the beginnings of time and find out why these creatures obey urges that today seem beyond reason, urges that were implanted in their genetic structure long before they came to present environments. In the case of the eelpout, a relative of the salt-water cod, it may have been that eons ago it was trapped in the north when the sea that brought it in finally retreated. Perhaps it came in the arm of the sea that laid down the iron deposits of the Mesabi, perhaps from one of the great extensions of glacial waters from the north. Whatever the cause of its introduction, somehow the species managed to survive, adapted itself gradually to the lack of salinity and the shallower depths of inland lakes, changed its habits of feeding and migration; instead of spawning on the ocean reefs it once frequented, it found it could survive by using open streams and the shallows of the lakes. It still keeps the ancient schedule, however, and spawns when the cod spawns in the sea, adhering that much to the age-old habits of the race.

The fish gradually became quiet and the brown eel-like shapes slipped away into the calmer waters below the riffle. There we could see them lying in the shadows, fanning the water with their long finned tails, waiting lazily until the strange apparitions and the unwelcome lights should go away.

This was a vital task that brooked no interruption. It was far more important than feeding or any other activity. As with all species, the entire life history led up to this supreme event. It was the climax of existence, the ultimate biological experience toward which everything previous was merely a preparation. When the crucial time was at hand, nothing must ever interfere for long. Like the trout, the salmon, and the eel, these fish had come from the depths to spawn where they themselves had first known the quickening of life. Each year for untold centuries the eelpout had come out of the lake to this particular place and at this very time. Each female left up to half a million or more of some of the smallest eggs produced by fish of inland waters. No wonder the rapids were colored by their release.

The turbulence had ceased and the fish lay furtively in the pool below. We had stopped them in the midst of their ritual, but they would begin again as soon as we were gone. A few nights more and they would swim back into the depths to wait another year before the urge took hold of them again. It was bitterly cold and we had been there for most of an hour. We dropped the flashlights into the pack, strapped on the skis, and pushed back on our trail to the open lake.

While hurrying across the moonlit ice, I could not erase from my mind what we had seen, something that might have taken place in a pool millions of years before. Here was life obeying the urge to reproduce, disregarding all else, bent only on fulfilling the ever implacable law of procreation.

For sheer primeval savagery, nothing I had ever seen compared to this. It seemed unreal as the river mouth grew dim behind us and the point ahead lay white and frosty under the moon. I felt somewhat uneasy, as though I had witnessed something I wasn't supposed to see, as though for a guilty moment I had peeked under the curtain at sheer brutality stripped of any of the beauty and joy and delight that is associated with the mating of the animals and birds I knew. Somehow it was as though I had done the unpardonable, stolen a look far back into the dim beginnings of life when forms on earth today were still eons from their origins.

We stopped at the end of the point and listened. We were warm now and our breath was frozen fog, and after we were quiet awhile we heard again the soft whisper of the rapids. The eelpout were back at their work, rolling over and over once more, twined around each other, slithering and slipping from one entangled group to another, beating the water white with their milt and eggs.

Perhaps it was the shape of the fish that affected me, the sinuous twisting forms reminding me of a nest of snakes I once had seen, a quivering mass of vipers. But even more was the feeling that I had watched some prehistoric scene, something from the age of fishes long before reptilian monsters ruled the earth, long before birds and mammals began their slow climb out of the primordial ooze. It was a strangely uncomfortable realization, and I almost wished I had not gone.

The mating of birds is a different thing, the pleasant happy nesting days of robins and bluebirds, of ducks and sparrows. There courtship means song and brilliant coloring and devotion of one mate to another. All mating until then had seemed a happy thing, but this was entirely different. Here was deadly seriousness, or so it seemed to me, a seriousness without music, romance, or joy, a powerful urge born of a force as inexorable as the turning of the spheres.

I felt much the same in the seal caves on the Oregon coast. It seemed then too as though I were looking far back into time at a scene that men had long forgotten. As I listened to the all-engulfing rush of the surf through the cave entrances and the roaring and barking of hundreds of seals, a sound magnified a thousand times by the cavern walls, I knew this was such a sound as ruled the earth long before the coming of man. I thought as I looked down the dim reaches of those cliff caves that nothing had changed there for millions of years and the traffic on the highway just above was but a temporary thing. That night too I was disturbed vaguely, for again I had lifted the veil and glimpsed the hidden past.

Another time, in the Florida Everglades, I listened to the rasping cough of alligators and the night screaming of countless birds, and as I lay there in the great swamp I was back in the primeval. That night the old hidden fears were with me, fears of the unknown that had lain deeply hidden in my subconscious.

We started a fire back on the beach, a great roaring fire, and threw on driftwood logs of cedar and pine. We sat before the blaze and toasted ourselves while the moonlight grew dim and the sparks flew high. Sitting there before the fire, what I had seen seemed not as awesome as before. Surely it was a glimpse into the past, but this I also knew: that out of that midnight breeding, out of the roaring seal caves of Oregon, and the sounds of the reptilian era down in the glades had come all of the life we know, all of the beauty we now take for granted, all of the song and gladness, as well as the mind of man, who could look at such things and give them meaning.

The next morning I sat in the sunlight in front of the cabin and listened to the merry song of the chickadees even though it was all of thirty below zero. I watched a red squirrel climb a jack pine and look for cones and then run around over the snow to find some it had cached. It was a bright sunlit frozen world again, and the spawning, while it still went on, seemed not as desperate as before.

The coffeepot was on in the fireplace, and wood smoke curled up into the still morning air. Sun dogs shone over the hills back of the beach, and trees cracked loudly with the frost. It was no time to be sitting outside even in the sun. This was a morning for reading and inviting one's soul. Later, when the crust was warmed, I might ski to a hole off one of the islands and try for a trout.

CHAPTER 26

BOBCAT TRAIL

The night after we had hauled in some logs for firewood was one of heavy snow. When I arrived at the point in the morning, the confusion of tracks and all signs of disturbance had disappeared and the big woodpile was a smooth unbroken mound. Nothing seemed to have moved since the storm.

I walked over to the bare rock just north of where the cabin was to be and looked out across the frozen expanse of the channel. It was then I noticed a set of tracks out on the ice, one single scar marring the glistening surface of the lake.

At first I thought the marks were deer tracks, but even at that distance I could see they were much too close together and compact, more likely a pair of coyotes or wolves. But as my eyes followed to where they entered the alder fringe below me, I saw by their roundness and regularity they were the tracks of two bobcats traveling side by side and heading for the rabbit country back of the point. Their trail passed between a juniper clump and a big white pine, then turned directly east.

This was late February and mating time, and the two were hunting together. Those tracks changed my plans for the day, and nothing seemed more important than following them. Lions, lynx, bobcats, leopards, tigers, and jaguars—all the variations of the breed have always intrigued the imaginations of men. While we think we know cats because of their long domesticity, this docile pet is still an enigma. You may understand dogs and horses and depend upon their loyalty, but a cat, never. It may seem reliable, constant, and affectionate, purr and snuggle when being fondled, but within it is a nature that has not changed since the days of the wild. The same beauty and grace, swift death and ferocity, and the all-knowing inscrutability typical of the species are still there.

I had seen evidence of deer and coyotes, mink and otter,

porcupines and rabbits on the point, but not a sign of the cats, though they were relatively plentiful and the area well within their range. I knew that, like the white-tailed deer, they had come originally from the open deciduous country of midcontinent, had during the past half-century gradually moved into the north, and were now found beyond the international border. When the great primeval forests began to fall, when the towering pines were replaced by aspen and birch, conditions became ideal for browsing types. It was then the deer moved in, replacing the caribou; and as rabbits increased because of unlimited food, the bobcats followed suit, replacing in turn their close relative the Canada lynx, which loved the gloom of conifers and moved northward away from the settlements.

This was good cat country now, open, broken ridges and swales, rocky slopes and cliffs, patches of virgin timber and second growth, the semi-open terrain they seem to need. Like the fox, the woodchuck and the raccoon, the bobcats had learned many clever tricks of survival, had established themselves in the new land and time and again extended their range as more and more country was opened up.

The realization that two of them had passed within fifty feet of the log pile and perhaps were hunting the ridges to the east no more than a mile away was all the incentive I needed. The fact that my chances of seeing them were slight did not dampen my resolve. In spite of their stealthy nocturnal habits and phenomenal eyesight, I just might be lucky, and, besides, there were many things to see along their hunting trail. Only once in my life had I seen a bobcat out of a trap or snare, and I have known many woodsmen in the north who have never even been that fortunate.

The trail led directly back of the point into the rocky aspen-grown ridges behind it. As I worked my way through the matted underbrush, I began to see signs of snowshoe rabbits, short foraging trails leading from beneath windfalls and the tunnels of snow-burdened branches bent to the ground. Tracks showed that the cats had investigated every sign, disappeared in tangled thickets, then emerged on the other side. Once I found where they had lain on a big log, for their bodies had melted the snow and several long hairs were frozen in the crust. Not once, however, did I find any trace of a kill or any serious hunting.

They had walked on either side of a small Norway to watch a porcupine feeding in its topmost branches. They could have climbed the tree easily and disemboweled the creature from underneath, toppled it to the snow, and gorged themselves to repletion, but that day they did not bother, and I began to suspect they were not too interested in food, that with the mating urge upon them they were content merely to roam together.

I followed the tracks into a dense swamp of cedar, black spruce, and balsam and in the half-light stood quietly for several minutes. In just juch a place, the favorite winter haunt of the bobcat, I had seen one years before. While following the trail of a deer and engrossed in unraveling the criss-crossed network of tracks, I had almost failed to see the cat crouched on a log not twenty feet away. It looked like an overgrown, mottled, reddish-brown tabby with tufted ears and a stubby tail. It was a big cat, for though the average is slightly less than three feet in length and twenty pounds in weight, they have been known to weigh thirty and even forty pounds. The Canada lynx may look like a much bigger cat, but it is only the extra length of fur, longer tufts on the ears, and bigger feet that give the impression of greater weight and size.

The cat sat on the log and watched me steadily, not stirring a muscle nor twitching a whisker, its great round eyes open wide, tufted ears erect. Somehow it did not seem very wild to me and I had the feeling I could stroke it if I had wished, but while I watched it slipped off the log and drifted like a shadow through the trees.

I waited in exactly the same kind of cover now, watching every log, suspicious of every flickering shadow. Near by on the snow were shredded bits of cedar bark, and I saw where one of them had reached up high and sharpened its claws on a tree as all cats do. A load of snow slid off a balsam branch with a sudden swish; I turned, and the branch moved slowly up and down. A raven flew overhead, so close I could hear the beating of its wings. A pair of whiskey-jacks discovered me, and their gray ghostly movements played havoc with my eyes. I stayed there for more than an hour until the cold began to penetrate, then moved on, following the tracks toward a great ridge north of the river, knowing that eventually the animals would swing back to the lake and not stray more than a few miles from where they had started.

Near the river, where the cats had skirted gingerly an open pool of water in a swamp, I met a woodsman cutting cedar poles.

"Keep after them critters," he said approvingly, "and you'll get thirty dollars bounty."

I did not tell him I was trailing the cats for fun, but let him feel that they belonged to me and that I planned to do exactly as he had suggested.

"Deer-killers," he added, looking closely at the trail. "Take a lot of partridge, too. Get rid of them and there'll be more deer and birds for everybody."

I knew that over a hundred thousand dollars had been paid in Minnesota in bounties on some eight thousand bobcats during the past five years, and although the number paid out during the last year of record was less than the first, the cats were still common and possibly always would be as long as second-growth aspen and birch provided browse for their favorite food, the snowshoe hare.

The woodsman believed all predators should be destroyed, a feeling many sportsmen share. Game biologists from all over the United States feel differently, for research has proven that the bulk of the food of the bobcat is rabbit, that they seldom eat deer meat except as carrion, and rarely kill game birds of any type. Regional studies in northern Minnesota indicate that ninety per cent of their food is composed of rabbit, carrion venison, and porcupine, with the remainder composed of practically anything they can find in the way of sustenance. Because the rabbit and porcupine compete with deer for food, many feel the bobcat should be protected, as it is one of the controlling factors of the smaller animals.

In the far north, records of the Hudson's Bay Company over a long period of time show that years of plenty as far as the rabbit is concerned are also years of plenty for the lynx. Years of scarcity due to the periodicity of disease cycles decimating the numbers of this source of food automatically reduce the cat population. The bobcat down below the range of the lynx is no exception to the rule.

The tracks began to circle, headed into the ridge country north of the river, climbed a high slope and wound in and out of huge broken boulders and blocks of fallen rock. I found a good vantage point and settled down to wait, watching through my field glasses for any movement that might betray the hunters. Anywhere in that tumbled confusion of snow-covered talus could be a resting-place. Aware that they never traveled more than five or six miles in any one night, that their hunting range is seldom greater in extent than can be covered in a single foray, I knew they had probably completed their circle by now, chosen their den site, and had gone back across the ice of the lake to their starting-point.

I saw a deer browsing in a clump of cedar at the base of the ridge and watched a pair of ravens soaring through the blue sky, circling and circling, looking for carrion. I began to think the birds had located a carcass, which might indicate the presence of the cats, but they finally swept grandly over the skyline and disappeared.

The ridge was a place the bobcats might well choose for the coming of their young around the middle of April. They would pick a sunny slope below the cliffs, preferably with big rocks and crevices, a windfall, a hollow log, or even a depression under a stump, some place where the den would be protected and the kittens could play undisturbed. In the country to the south they might pick a hollow tree, but in the north such places were rare. They would line the nest with grass or moss or leaves just as a house cat does in preparation for its young. The kittens would come as the ice was turning black on the lakes, when the creeks were running full and buds swelling. Usually two to four in number, they would roll and frolic as all kittens do and look no different from those we know, but most attempts to tame them have resulted in failure, for within those cuddly little balls of fur is a wildness that no amount of feeding or love can change.

Like the adults, they will puff their cheeks, growl and spit and scratch and prove without question that they have earned the name of wildcat. Nocturnal and furtive, seldom making a sound or showing any sign of emotion when left alone, they epitomize the untamed freedom of open country.

The day was warm, for it was the time of the February thaw with snow melting on the south slopes and dry brown places beginning to show. I sat on one of them beneath a small pine where the needles smelled of resin and the humus was almost soft.

I stayed there longer than I should have, basking in the sunshine and watching the ridge before me. When the cold settled down, I left my lookout, found the faded paw marks once more, and worked my way back to the shore of the lake. The sun was low as I started across the ice, and streamers of orange and pale green hung over the west. The new snow was packed firmly onto the crust, and it seemed good to travel without the encumbrance of brush or trees.

When I reached the point, I walked over to the rock where I had first seen the tracks some eight hours before, stood there in the dusk listening for a sound I had heard long ago and hoped to hear again, but now there was only the soft settling of the snow and the distant barking of a dog. An owl hooted back in the darkening timber, and I knew the rabbits in the aspen were cowering in their shelters. But I remembered vividly the one time I had heard the yowling of a bobcat, a sound that made such an impression on me that I have never forgotten it.

It was on a canoe trip in the Ansellette country to the north, and we were camped in a great swampy area with broken rocky ridges and slopes. On a night that was black and still I wakened before dawn and walked down to the water's edge, where I stood listening. From the dark and silent timber of the opposite shore came a half-choked screaming sound with the most frightening variations I had ever heard. Not until I recalled the caterwauling of an old tom back of the garden fence did my equanimity return. Here was the same awful medley, only magnified and a thousand times more impressive because of the absolute stillness. I listened in amazement and delight as echoes filled the little bay with their full and horrible crescendo.

Some black night when all is still, it might come again, and Listening Point will be the richer for the sound. Even knowing the possibility meant much to me, for, like all the music of the wilds, this had meaning too. Some night toward the end of winter or in the early spring I might hear it once more, and for that I will stand and listen in the years to come.

CHAPTER 27

PUSSY WILLOWS

THE crust had been firm for a month. In the mornings before the sun was high you could walk anywhere without sinking in, and on skis you could all but fly through the open woods with a freedom of movement unknown during the soft heavy snows of winter. But along the south exposures of the hills, where the brown was showing through, disaster lurked in the shape of bare rocks and snares of hazel and maple looped flat to the ground by the pressure of the drifts. There the skis were better carried, so I took them off and headed for the road on foot.

It was then I met three little girls wandering along the highway. I could see at once they were on an important mission that April morning, for the instant they saw me they hurried over and one of them said: "Can you tell us where we can find some pussy willows?"

That question was too delightful to ignore, for pussy willows are important in the spring. In a world seething with mistrust, suspicion and clashing ideologies, pussy willows may be vital to the welfare of man and his serenity. My explorers could not possibly know the real significance of their search or its far-reaching implications, but that made little difference.

I took them in tow and soon found a bush coming nicely into bloom. While they waited on the road, I plowed through the snow and picked some of the silver pussies from the sunlit tops, saw that each had an ample bouquet, and sent them happily on their way.

"Thank you," they called as they headed down the highway, "thank you for the pussies." I watched them until they disappeared around a bend. The chickadees sang more gaily than before, and the patches of snow sparkled with even a brighter morning light.

There was no need to thank me, for they brought back in a flash the days of my own boyhood when the finding of the first pussies in the spring was the most exciting event of the year. Those softly furred silver buds emerging miraculously from brown shiny scales while snow was still on the ground told me more than all other signs of spring, for they were the real beginnings, the first intimations of stirring life in the long-frozen north.

I have learned much about the botanical nature of willows since those early days, know now which bushes are male and which female, have dissected staminate and pistilate flowers, know how the tiny seeds develop and the parachute down that sends them eventually far from the parent bush in search of places to germinate. I have discovered that there are many kinds, some three hundred species, subspecies and hybrids scattered all over the world except in Australia and New Zealand. I know too that the willow has a rather lax morality when it comes to maintaining its purity, crossing not only with related types but with dwarf birches as well to the point where its classification has become such a nightmare of involved and varying characters one may easily lose sight of its beauty and the part it plays in the life of mankind and the creatures dependent upon it.

Wherever there is water you find it, even in high mountains, and in the far north Salix Arctica has the distinction of being one of the few woody plants in a land where trees are almost unknown. Along thousands of creeks and rivulets, sloughs and ponds and the forgotten watercourses of the tundra, the willow grows luxuriously, providing fuel for native tribes, browse for moose and caribou. Beside the canals beavers have dug from ponds to stands of aspen, willows serve as screens against enemies.

Where the rivers are swift, the long fibrous roots entwined around particles of soil prevent erosion. Its shade on little streams slows evaporation, keeps temperatures down where spring-fed trickles fan out into the hot sunlight of meadows and brook trout dart like shadows from bank to bank.

In the south the willows grow large, and in many sections of the old world the process of pollarding or cutting off each year's growth for firewood and elastic withes for baskets and ties in the culture of grapes has made the resulting rounded form a common feature of the landscape. Even on some islands of Lake Erie, where grapes are grown for wine, this ancient custom prevails.

Destined for common things and common enjoyments, the willow plays a role unheralded and unsung. Of no value as lumber because of the softness of its wood and its erratic growth, it need never face extinction. It competes with no plants of economic importance, threatens the survival of no species, occupies areas where little else will grow. Perhaps as important a function as any is the joy the willow brings each spring when it bursts into bloom all over the world and heralds the approach of another season.

When my young friends asked me where the pussies grew, I knew theirs would be a joy particularly indigenous to willows. While I might understand the genus more, they would

have an uncluttered sense of pleasure uninfluenced by knowledge. In this day of knowing a little about everything, that
was very important.

After the sound of their small happy voices was gone, I
abandoned all I had planned for the day, convinced there
were other things to do. My visitors had launched me on a
type of research that would go on for weeks. While it might
not add anything to the sum total of man's knowledge, my
eyes had been opened anew to joy and wonder and a fresh
realization of a great phenomenon, the surging impatience
of all forms of life to exchange their cells even before the
snows were gone and the earth had warmed. All the great
trees, all the shrubs were waiting, and some that could not
wait had already begun. The pussy willows were the van-
guard, but there were others too if only I could find them.
The coming days would be dedicated to the search and to a
study of pussy willows and their relationship to what was
happening all around me.

The crust softened swiftly under the sun, and soon it was
impossible to step anywhere without sinking clear to the
ground. The ice of the bay, though darkening fast, was solid
as it had ever been, but along the shore on the south side of
the point was already a narrow strip of open water. I looked
at it in amazement, for it was the first I had seen. Brown
leaves swayed gently in its flow. How clear it was and how
beautiful the pebbles underneath. That tiny strip of water
seemed alive, and I lay down and put my face in it and took
a long drink and watched the bottom as through a glass.

Soon the strip would widen, the ice become honeycombed and then disappear beneath the waves.

Two weeks later, against the ledge of greenstone there and just above the water, I found a hazel bush as gray and wiry as in the fall, still beaten to the ground as it was at the base of the ridge along the ski trail. One branch flat against the rock was in full bloom, and I found a cluster of the Y-shaped pistils of the female flower peeking like a tiny crimson brush between the drab brown scales protecting it. I broke off a tip and examined it closely, studied the bloom not more than an eighth of an inch in length, saw how waxy and finely made it was and how gemlike against the gray-green background of the ledge. These tiny Y's of ruby were not meant for insect pollination, depended entirely on gravity and on the wind. I shook the little branch against the rock and watched the drifting down of the golden pollen grains from the male catkins into the open throats of the waiting pistils below, saw how infallibly they caught their share and more.

A little farther on I found a swamp maple with one branch on the sunny side responding to warmth in the same way, its flowers more gorgeous and elaborate, the clustered panicles of bells, male and female, in a single flower bright enough to attract the wasps. Though early, far too early, it seemed to me, I could already hear their buzzing, but even without them the wind would take care of pollination as it did with the willow and the hazel.

I picked a single spray and saw how the pollen stalks raised themselves above the sunken pistils of the females, how instantly when the pollen was released and showered down, the dust settled on them and stayed. The topmost branch was rosy with bloom, a hint of what would come when the new leaves burst out of their gray covering of scales and what the fall held in store as well. For the maples of the swamps usher in the seasons with the same mist of color with which they bow them out. I touched the broken end of the branch with my tongue and tasted the sweetness of sap already beginning to flow.

A squirrel leaped from a pine near by, scrambled up into the maple tree, nibbled a couple of blossoms, swiftly found the broken branch, and tasted the sweetness as I had done a moment before.

It was early for the pines, but perhaps on some protected branch on the south slope of the ridge where the sun had really done its work, I would find what I sought. I followed the trail back toward the road, and in a hot little pocket where a pine nestled close to a cleft in the rock I discovered a single branch with purple staminate clusters as beautiful as any flower in the north. Within a few weeks the air would be heavy with drifting pollen and the whole north country covered with a golden cloud from all the pines a hundred miles around. So dense and widespread would be its drift that even the lakes would look as though in bloom, and along the beaches would be a golden line where the pollen had washed ashore.

Again the tiny female flowers were hidden beneath drab

protecting scales, but the shower of fertilizing cells would find them out and begin the growth that after two long years would produce seed cones in the tops and at the ends of branches.

All that day I hunted for the first flowers of shrubs and trees, found the bronze pendant catkins of alder, the swelling buds of moosewood, rubbed the great resinous leaf buds of Balm of Gilead in my hand and smelled a fragrance that soon would drench the woods with richness. I sat on top of the ridge and saw the faint blush of purple in the tops of birches, the glow of dogwoods in a bog, warming colors that presaged the coming change.

None of the blossoms I had found were as well known as the herbaceous types which soon would bloom on the forest floor, but seeing them before they were lost in the avalanche of coming leaves was important. How I wished my young friends of the pussy willows could have seen the ruby pistils of the hazel, the rosy sunbursts of maple, and the purple of the pine. They had asked for pussies because these they knew, but had they known the others, their joy would have been even greater than mine, for spring was in their eyes and they could see them as they should be seen.

I walked out to the end of the point and looked over the lake. It was blue and sparkling now and the ice was long forgotten. A purple finch was back, one of the first, and its liquid rippling notes sounded from the pale-green ridges behind me. The air was full of new smells and the sounds of open water. Myriads of growing things were now forcing themselves up through the mold. Swiftly now and the woods would be full of bloom and the tree flowers forgotten.

What I had seen so far was merely a prelude of what was to come. But more than the pussy willows that had initiated my research was the joy I had seen in the eyes of three little girls. They had taught me again that such things were important, had reminded me it was time to look around before the hidden beauties of sunny slopes were lost in the wilderness of green to come.

CHAPTER 28

FAR HORIZONS

WE HAD climbed the ridge in back of the point, the old lumberjack and I, and stood there on a bare ledge of rock looking out toward the blue horizons across the lake. Beyond and to the north was the unbroken wilderness of lakes and rivers known as the Quetico-Superior.

"I like this place," said my friend. "Don't know how to

explain it exactly, but I like the feeling of looking a long way without seeing any houses."

The Canadian French had a name for what he felt and what all men feel at times. *"Pays d'en haut,"* they called it, the land of lakes, rivers, and forests beyond the settlements, the lure that had dominated their lives for almost three hundred years in their explorations of the unmapped continent from Montreal and Quebec to the barren lands of the arctic and as far as the western sea. Back in the days of early colonization those three words explained the virtual abandonment of farms and villages by the adventurous *voyageurs* who had listened to a siren call more powerful than the ties of civilization or the bonds of family.

The lumberjack was no different. What had kept him in the woods following the river drives and the logging operations from Maine to the lake states was more than freedom and the love of adventure. It was the same challenge of far horizons he had known and the shared realization that once you have seen the blue and known the wilderness, nothing else is worth while.

I left him there smoking his pipe contentedly and strolled back to the point where I could look across to the islands. Here was my own particular "back of beyond," and as long as the point was mine it would never change. Though someone might build on one of those islands, the development would be far enough away so it could never be seen clearly. Nothing would ever destroy this lookout point of mine to the undeveloped north.

The sun had set and the west was a wild and angry red with scudding clouds and whitecaps beating across the channel. No one would be out on a night like this, for the gale was insulation against the outside world, and the point was as alone and as much a part of solitude as before it had been discovered. I sat there in the teeth of the wind, watching the flaming combers grow dark and menacing. On one such night not long ago I had watched a sunset on the Churchill far to the north, had sat on another rock and listened to the huskies tuning up around an Indian camp and had felt the immensity and loneliness of great forgotten waterways.

Others might find their *"pays d'en haut"* in tiny hidden corners where through accident or design a breath of the primeval has been saved, but, like the lumberjack with memories of far horizons he had known, such places were never quite enough for me. I remembered a little creek within the city limits of Washington, D.C., where within a stone's throw of the traffic the roar seemed to merge with the chuckle of running water and the whisper of a breeze in the tall trees. Down below in the cool green twilight, the air vibrant with the hum of insects and the calling of birds, one could sense for a moment what must have been in Rock Creek Valley a hundred years ago.

I thought of the waterfront of Chicago, where, shielded only by a ledge from the famous outer drive and the traffic of one of the busiest metropolitan cities in the world, is a place where one can look out to the open lake and catch a sense of distance and space. Each time I am in the city I go there and for a little while hold the vision, but then my years in the bush crowd upon me and I long for the great silences away from the towns.

And so it must be for all of us who have known the back country. No little sanctuaries along the fringes of civilization ever quite suffice. We must know the wild and all it entails, the bite of a tumpline on the portages, the desperate battling on stormy lakes, the danger and roar of rapids and falls. We must know hunger and thirst and privation and the companionship of men on the outtrails of the world, for all these things are inseparable. When after days or weeks of travel we modern voyageurs find ourselves on a glaciated point a hundred or a thousand miles from any town and stand there gazing down the length of some unnamed lake listening to the wild calling of the loons and watching the islands floating in the sunset, there is a fierce joy in our hearts.

Some find their wilderness in the grandeur of snow-capped peaks and high flowering meadows. To mountain men this is the primeval on a noble scale, a timelessness and immensity they seem to find nowhere else. They come down from the hills, as men have always done, refreshed and ready once more for life among their kind.

There are those who say that only in the great swamps and flowages of the deep south or the tropics can one understand what the primeval really means, and in a sense they are right, for it was in such places that life supposedly evolved. The lush rain forests of the Pacific coast are much the same, with high sunlight shading into the perpetual twilight of the forest floor. There too one has the sense of being at one with the life that has produced so lavishly.

There are the oceans, the deserts and the barren lands, all places where physical barriers have kept man and his ingenuity from penetrating the frontiers they represent. As long as they remain, as long as there are any places left at all where man can still glimpse the unknown, he will be drawn irresistibly as he has been for ages past, and, seeing them, will wonder and dream and think long thoughts.

The dusk was settling, the crescendo of waves against the rocks becoming more menacing than ever. I could feel the spray, moved to the bearberry patch just beyond it, lit a fire behind a rock and brewed a pot of tea. Out there in the storm was what all of them had known, what explorers and adventurers had gone to the ends of the earth to find, there the compelling reason for all expeditions no matter where they might be and for all the searching of men for the quiet the race had once known.

The fact that relatively few have any intimate physical contact with undeveloped country is unimportant. While traveling by canoe, packhorse, or on foot may be the ideal way to experience the wilds, the very existence of such areas affects those who see only its fringes or are aware that it exists at all. So ingrained in our consciousness, so intuitive is this reaction that even a suggestion of wilderness adds richness and color to experience.

The many millions who drive through our national parks and forests, though they may never set foot on any of the

239

back-country trails, never know the wilderness except from their automobiles, nevertheless are conscious of its power, a realization that gives significance to everything they see. The lure is more than scenery, varied vistas and magnificent lookout points; it is the consciousness of being at the threshold of the unknown.

Stephen Leacock, the Canadian humorist, when asked why he persisted in living in Toronto instead of his much lauded England, replied that in Canada he always felt close to the bush, that the very thought of the millions of square miles of wild country to the north gave him an expansiveness of soul he could find nowhere else.

My little fire fought for its life behind the rock, and I crouched there drinking the last cup of tea and listened to the wind roaring through the pines and the waves crashing against the rocks. That moment I was as alone and as much a part of the wilderness as I had ever been.

As I sat there I thought I knew what Leacock had really meant. In his reply he recognized the awe and wonderment of the unknown that over the uncounted centuries of man's development may have given rise to the first vague intimations of religious feeling, to the rude sketches on the walls of caves, to the eternal striving for understanding of the universe. If far horizons gave him an expansiveness of soul, it might well be it was part of the great urge of all men to penetrate the blue frontiers, that in their instinctive curiosity to know what lay beyond was one of the creative forces that lifted man from the dark abyss of the primitive to a state of growing perception.

The little flame of my fire had died into a glowing bed of coals with flecks of white ash around the edges. I tossed on a handful of pine needles and tiny sticks, and for a moment they flared. I gazed into the coals as men have done for a hundred thousand years. There in the gloom nothing had changed at all. A horned owl hooted back in the timber, knowing nothing of my thoughts. The wild and stormy night was music, a good night for the hunting down of prey.

Though to modern man the music seems to have changed, he still listens to the ancient rhythms. His are the old fears as well as the basic satisfactions, and because of them there is a powerful nostalgia for the wild. While the great silences are now shattered by the roar of jets, the cities he has built vibrating with noise, natural smells replaced by those of combustion and industry, senses bombarded with new and violent impressions, he is still attuned to woods and fields and waters. He has come a long way from the primitive, but not far enough to forget. Were it not for a nature steeped in a racial experience that knew nothing of these things, his adjustment might be swift, but adaptations take eons of time, and mental and physiological processes that have been maturing slowly for a million years cannot be ignored at will. Man of the Atomic Age and its conflicting ideologies is still part of the past.

I warmed my hands over the dying fire. The ledge on

which it glowed was over three billion years of age. The greenstone had been there almost that long before man first appeared on earth. Then for unknown ages after that he lived the life of a primitive while all the sights and sounds and smells of his environment were stored in a great subconscious pool of experience. He was of the wild and the wild of him, and so completely was he part of it that ages could not change him. So recent was his final emergence from the dark of the Stone Age and his endless nomadic wanderings that in the evolutional time-clock of life it was barely an instant.

Even a century ago he lived close to the soil, and though drastic changes were on the way, he was still at one with the out-of-doors. Then almost without warning he was hurled into the whirring complexities of the machine age and found himself removed from any direct contact with the life he had known, discovered he could live without having to hunt for food, gather wood, carry water, or till the soil, that matters of security and community welfare were taken care of by those who were seldom seen. After eons of insecurity, danger, and fear, he believed the millennium had come, but strangely enough found something missing, that in spite of new comforts and pleasures he was confused, distraught, and sometimes unhappy. Instinctively he looked backward, sensing vaguely what he had lost, and discovered that in far horizons, wherever they might be, was a partial answer to the hunger and unrest within him.

And so it will be for centuries to come. Men will always be drawn to the last frontiers, where they can recapture some of the basic satisfactions and joys of the race, renew the sense of mystery and wonder and even some of the dreams their forebears had known. Some will embark on wilderness expeditions, but most will content themselves with a fleeting look at places that are still wild and unchanged. Even those who cannot travel will gain comfort from knowing far horizons are there.

The storm was still raging, and though I could no longer see the whitecaps, the point was alive with their crashing and the hiss of them as they broke over the ledge. I threw on another handful of needles and in the flash of flame caught for an instant the white crest of a comber and then it was darker than before.

A NOTE ABOUT THE AUTHOR

SIGURD F. OLSON was born in Chicago in 1899. His family moved to northern Wisconsin in 1905. A graduate of the University of Wisconsin, he also pursued post-graduate work there in geology, supplementing it with advanced studies in plant and animal ecology at the University of Illinois. For a number of years he taught biology at Ely Junior College (Minnesota), where he later was dean. He has been recognized nationally with many awards and honorary degrees and has served as consultant to the federal government on wilderness preservation and ecological problems, as adviser to the Izaak Walton League of America, and as president of the Wilderness Society and the National Parks Association. His books include *The Singing Wilderness* (1956), *Listening Point* (1958), *The Lonely Land* (1961), *Runes of the North* (1963), and *Open Horizons* (1969). A season-by-season selection of his writings, *Sigurd F. Olson's Wilderness Days*, was published in 1972. Interpreter, enjoyer—and conserver—of our natural heritage, he lives and works in Ely, Minnesota, gateway to the Quetico-Superior region.